A FAITHFUL HEART

A
Faithful Heart
Daily Guide for Joyful Living

SALLY DYCK

ABINGDON PRESS
Nashville

A FAITHFUL HEART
DAILY GUIDE FOR JOYFUL LIVING

ISBN 978-1-4267-0998-2

10 11 12 13 14 15 16 17 18 19—10 9 8 7 6 5 4 3 2 1
MANUFACTURED IN THE UNITED STATES OF AMERICA

Contents

Introduction

What is a faithful heart? And where do I get one?

Through this resource, you may be surprised to discover that you already have a faithful heart, one that simply desires to grow in faithfulness, love, and joy. As you read, you will identify the characteristics of a faithful heart and recognize how to strengthen these in your daily living as well. You will discover that a faithful heart is, and is always striving to be,

> *Passionate*
> *Called*
> *Holy*
> *Equipped*
> *Joyful*
> *Loving*
> *Learning*
> *Authentic*

In this book, I have used one of my favorite biblical characters—Mary, the mother of Jesus—as an example of someone with a faithful heart. Too often Mary gets lost in the nativity scene and is shrouded with all kinds of doctrinal questions. We lose sight of her growing, faithful heart as she trusted

God in bearing Christ into the world, learned from Jesus throughout his earthly ministry, and was counted among his followers in the early church.

There are other women—in my life and yours, too—who demonstrate a faithful heart. When we remember and recite their faithfulness, our own faith is strengthened. When we share our faith, others' hearts are strengthened. A faithful heart is one that is willing to stretch, grow, and share.

While this resource can be used by the individual for personal meditation, study, and prayer, I encourage you to draw together a few friends or invite others in your church to join you as spiritual companions to share insights, ask questions, and probe further in the areas of the spiritual journey.

One sign of a faithful heart is, I believe, a joyful life. A joyful life doesn't mean that we're happy all the time but rather that we are closely connected to God and others so that throughout the events of our lives we have the heart to face life's many demands and to appreciate the goodness in life with a sense of God's presence and support of others.

I trust that as you read, study, and meditate on the theme each week, you'll discover a growing, faithful heart in yourself and each other and experience the practices that give us daily joy.

Sally Dyck

Passionate:
Beloved of God

passionate

Challenge for Week 1

This week, as you find yourself in an ordinary place or surrounding, practice seeing the presence of God. Recall what you see or sense, and journal about it or share the experience with a loved one or someone in the group.

Week One
Passionate:
Beloved of God

Do you see God in your life every day?

*W*hen we can sense and feel and therefore know the presence of God, it is the tangible presence of God in our lives. We touch, feel, perceive, sense, recognize, and notice God around and within us; God's presence is something that is obvious, evident, and plain. I want a passionate faith where I deeply sense God's presence in my life.

Passionate is a confusing word, especially for people who are introverted. Passionate often implies a proscribed way in which one experiences God: a jumping up and down, raising your hands, and shouting out loud way of experiencing God. That may be unfair to the word *passionate*; its true meaning describes something that is ardent, fervent, and deeply felt. I want to deeply feel and experience God's presence. I want my expression of it to be authentic to whatever it is that I perceive, sense, and notice about God's presence in my life. Today. Any day. Any time.

But why is it that sometimes we feel the presence of God and sometimes we don't? Why is it that some people seemingly sense God's presence in their lives more readily than others?

N. Graham Standish suggests that just as there are multiple intelligences, such as emotional, musical, and intellectual intelligences—or ways of knowing—so there is a mystical intelligence "which has to do with how aware we are of God's purpose, presence, and power."[1] It's intriguing to think that just as people have varying degrees of intellectual, emotional, musical, and other intelligences, so we might also have a varying degree of mystical intelligence. A mystical intelligence simply means that we have a way of knowing God's presence through our mind, our senses, our feelings, and our intuition.

Initially it might sound like we either have it or we don't, but Standish doesn't describe it that way. Likewise, the theory of multiple intelligences doesn't suggest that we either have one or another, but that we have a degree of any of the intelligences and we can cultivate them in our lives so as to enhance our ways of knowing, learning, and experiencing life.

Throughout our readings, journaling, and prayer this week, we will explore the ways in which we experience the palpable, passionate presence of God in life's situations, look for God's goodness even when life is difficult and stressful, and seek God's will in our lives.

---

[1] N. Graham Standish, *Humble Leadership: Being Radically Open to God's Guidance and Grace* (The Alban Institute, 2007); p. 142.

You Are Beloved by God

*In the sixth month the angel Gabriel was sent by God to
a town in Galilee called Nazareth, to a virgin engaged to
a man whose name was Joseph, of the house of David.
The virgin's name was Mary. And he came to her and
said, "Greetings, favored one! The Lord is with you!"*
(Luke 1:26-28)

*M*ary experienced the passionate presence of God in a
messenger, Gabriel. In a specific time, in a specific re-
gion and town, a woman with a specific name and family
connections received a message. In her everyday, ordinary
life, God was present to Mary and God's presenting message
to Mary was that she was beloved (or favored) and that God
was with her. Repeat after me:

I, (your name)_____, am beloved by God,
and God is with me today!

Later when Jesus was baptized, he too heard the voice of God saying, "You are my Son, the Beloved; with you I am well pleased" (Luke 3:22). God doesn't send us out into our everyday lives without the assurance that we're beloved and that God is with us to face the events of our lives.

Messengers of God's love don't usually appear before us as celestial beings with gigantic wings. They are usually people that God sends our way with the message that we are loved, appreciated, and respected.

My Reflections

Who are the messengers of God's love in your life?

To whom can you be a messenger of God's love?

Day

2

Surely the Presence of the Lord Is in This Place

*"So here's what I want you to do, God helping you: Take
your everyday, ordinary life—your sleeping, eating,
going-to-work, and walking-around life—and place it
before God as an offering. Embracing what God does for
you is the best thing you can do for [God]." (Romans
12:1-2, The Message)*

Experiencing the passionate presence of God means
that we seek to sense, notice, and perceive God
around us. We stop confining God to some activities, such
as going to church, reading the Bible, and praying, and
begin to sense God's presence in anything or anywhere.

As Eugene Peterson in his paraphrase of Romans 12 calls it,
giving my "everyday, ordinary life" as an offering to God

means that God meets me where I'm at whether or not it's a place I would expect to see or experience God. It means that as a result of God meeting me where I'm at, God transforms the way I see the world around me—my friends and family as well as strangers, my work and daily tasks of life, the beauty of creation, and the world's suffering.

It's pretty easy for me to see God in the face of a child, a loved one, or someone I'm called to serve (well, mostly). But sometimes it's the stranger's face that proves difficult for me, or the awkward and painful experience. But if in fact we can cultivate a mystical intelligence, then we need to practice seeing God wherever we are.

One day I was flying to attend a meeting, and there was a layover at an airport that got extended due to bad weather. I had gotten up early that morning to catch my flight, so I hadn't had the opportunity to go for my regular morning run. As a result, I hadn't gone through my prayer routine, which I do while running. So I decided to "walk" the airport, saying my prayers silently as I did.

As I was praying, I began to sing (in my mind, I assure you), "Surely the Presence of the Lord Is in This Place."[2] Why did that song come into my mind in the midst of a busy, crowded airport?

"Surely the presence of the Lord is" in the meadow where I normally run and where I had recently come upon two white-tailed deer as they galloped parallel to me on the edge of the meadow near the woods. Surely the presence of the Lord is there.

"I can feel [God's] mighty power and [God's] grace" in the beauty of the sunrise, the beautiful flowering trees, or even the pristine snow-covered woods; but here in a busy, crowded airport?

"I can hear the brush of angels' wings" in the wind in the trees, the song of the birds, and the running creek that I cross, but here in a busy, crowded airport? Angels' wings here? Frankly, when you're flying, you don't want to think about hearing angels' wings!

"I see glory on each face." Suddenly, when those words came to my mind, I began to see the people around me . . . differently. People were coming and going, some undoubtedly sad as they headed for a funeral, and others joyous as they anticipated reunions with family and friends. Business people were talking frantically on their phones as their planes were delayed or canceled. A mother with five children under the age of six, elderly people and folks with broken legs being transported in wheelchairs, people of all sizes and shapes and colors as well as people who appeared to represent many different religions comprised the busy, crowded airport.

Suddenly I began to recognize the presence of the Lord in that place and on their faces! God is present in unlikely places, busy places, and places where we might not expect to see or recognize God.

[2] "Surely the Presence of the Lord Is in This Place," words and music by Lanny Wolfe, *The United Methodist Hymnal* (The United Methodist Publishing House); p. 328.

My Reflections

When have you seen the presence of God in an ordinary place or experience in life?

Where do you need to practice seeing the presence of God?

Day

3

Expecting God

"So if you're serious about living this new resurrection life with Christ, act like it. Pursue the things over which Christ presides. Don't shuffle along, eyes to the ground, absorbed with the things right in front of you. Look up, and be alert to what is going on around Christ—that's where the action is. See things from his perspective. Your old life is dead. Your new life, which is your real life— even though invisible to spectators—is with Christ in God. He is your life." (Colossians 3:1-3, The Message)

n Graham Standish describes one of the elements of mystical intelligence as "an acceptance and expectation of providence."[3] Mystical intelligence is simply a way of describing how we have a way of knowing God's presence through our mind, our senses, our feelings, and even our intuition. When we cultivate a sense of God's presence in our lives, we look for God all around us and expect to see and experience God's goodness in our lives and world.

I heard about a woman who would take her dog for a walk each morning. As they were walking through a grove of trees, a squirrel fell out of the tree right in front of the dog. Dog heaven! But the remarkable thing about the experience was that on subsequent walks, every time they came to that place in the grove of trees, the dog would perk up with expectation and literally quiver with anticipation that something good could happen!

In a sense, that's what it means to expect that God provides goodness in our lives. We look for the goodness, even when we experience suffering or tragedy. Years ago my extended family experienced a horrible tragedy that resulted with two members of our family dying. It was a devastating experience that forever impacted us.

But as we prepared for this double funeral, my mother shared a list she had made of how God had been in the midst of it. My definition of tragedy is that God doesn't intend for it to happen—I would never say that God willed or intended for this tragedy to happen—but I believe in the midst of the worst of life, even in dying, God is present and sometimes even more palpable because in our darkest times we look for every glimmer of light.

God's goodness may be in the silence rather than the speech, in the edges rather than the center of things, in the healing rather than the untouched.

[3] Standish; p. 148.

My Reflections

When do you expect, even anticipate, that you will experience the goodness of God?

When have you experienced the passionate, felt presence of God in the midst of life's worst?

Day

4

Being Reminded of God's Goodness

*"Open your mouth and taste, open your eyes
and see—how good God is.
Blessed are you who run to him."*
(Psalm 34:8, The Message)

Three women—a Muslim, a Jew, and a Christian—came together after 9/11 to better understand each other's faiths. In the process, each of them experienced a deepening of her faith. Priscilla Warner, the Jewish woman in the triad, was standing in line for pizza one day when she thought about how her journey with these other two women had taken her to new and unexpected places in her spiritual life. She felt a sense of God's presence in her life in a real and personal way. The presence of God was as perceptible as the smell of the tomato sauce! It nearly overcame her and brought tears to her eyes as she contemplated a sense of God's goodness in her life in so many ways.

Right in the pizza shop, she began to recite a "personal credo," what she believed about the goodness of God:

> I believe that God is the goodness that exists inside each and every human being, every animal, every flower, and every miracle of God's creation. I believe that God is a force that binds us together, showing up in the moments when people make unexpected, magical connections with each other. God challenges us, I believe, to become our best selves, even in the toughest times, when beauty and goodness seem to be mysteriously elusive, overshadowed by excruciating pain and evil.[4]

I would describe this as a mystical experience or even a religious experience that spoke to her in a life-changing way. Right there in a pizza shop! "I will do my very best to enjoy my life," she promised herself, a person who was often anxious and worried about many things.[5]

---

[4] Ranya Idliby, Suzanne Oliver, and Priscilla Warner, *The Faith Club: A Muslim, a Christian, a Jew—Three Women Search for Understanding* (Free Press, 2006); p. 267.
[5] *The Faith Club*; p. 268.

My Reflections

Have you ever been "filled up" with a sense of the goodness of life and God? Where were you when this happened?

Are you someone who is often anxious and worried about many things? What's a reminder of God's goodness in your daily life that could help you do your very best to enjoy life?

Day

5

The Quilt of Your Life

"We know that all things work together for good for those who love God, who are called according to his purpose." (Romans 8:28)

Standish cites another element of mystical intelligence as "a passionate desire to make God's will a priority."[6] We may strongly desire God's will in our lives, but we don't always know what it is or how to figure it out. We might feel like there's only one path, yet so many people I know have taken some detours along the way to getting where they are that it's hard to believe that the detours aren't part of the path! I believe that God's will is that we take what we have in life and make something of it that is good and pleasing to ourselves, to others, and also to God—an offering of our lives to those around us and God.

Eliza Calvert Hall wrote a best-selling novel in 1907, entitled *Aunt Jane of Kentucky*. The main character, Aunt Jane Parrish, seeks and reflects on the everyday tasks that women do, especially the task of quilting, in such a way that speaks to larger meanings in life. In a dialogue between Aunt Jane and her niece, she makes this observation:

> "Did you ever think, child, how much piecin' a quilt's like livin' a life?" Aunt Jane asks her niece. Then she explains in plain, heartfelt language about picking out calico, "caliker," and patterns. A firm believer in free will, Aunt Jane makes a case that every person is in charge of her own life, whatever fate the Lord provides. "The Lord sends us the pieces," Aunt Jane goes on, "but we can cut 'em and put 'em together pretty much to suit ourselves, and there's a heap more in the cuttin' out and the sewin' than there is in the caliker."[7]

Aunt Jane seems to be suggesting that God gives us the "pieces" of our lives—our childhood experiences, the formative years of our faith, our relationships, where we live, when we live, our physical bodies and the joys and challenges they present us with, our interests and our personalities shaped by nature and nurture, the people throughout our lives. The whole package of pieces then is ours to put together into a life of meaning and purpose.

Furthermore, the Amish believe that in every quilt given to newlyweds, there must be darker, more somber tones to remind the couple that not all of life is going to happy. So our "caliker" is both bright and somber.

[6] Standish; p. 151.
[7] *A Quilter's Wisdom: Conversations With Aunt Jane*, Based on a text by Eliza Calvert Hall, Introduction by Roderick Kiracofe (Chronicle Books, 1994); p. viii.

My Reflections

What colors dominate the quilt of your life?

What are some of the pieces that you are so grateful that are in your quilt of life?

Which ones have been more of a challenge for you to cut, sew, and arrange in your quilt of life?

Day

6

Holy Is...

God said, "I am holy; you be holy."
(1 Peter 1:15, The Message*)*

Singer and songwriter Carrie Newcomer, in her song
"Holy as a Day Is Spent," describes all the little things
she experiences daily—the dishes, warm socks, busy streets,
shaking hands, and quiet moments—as being holy,

> It's all a part of a sacrament
> as holy as the day is spent . . . [8]

It's sometimes difficult to think of each day as holy, when
days are filled with checking off the to-do list, isn't it? Again
we recall Eugene Peterson's paraphrase of Romans 12, "Take
your everyday, ordinary life—your sleeping, eating, going-
to-work, and walking-around life—and place it before God
as an offering." Our everyday, ordinary lives are offerings to
God.

Newcomer concludes her song saying that every morning "sings providence." If we think of our days as being divinely guided, or full of "providence," this changes our perspective on the to-do list. Folding the laundry can become a blessing to your family, shaking someone's hand could be the physical touch that person needs to feel connected to something greater, a quiet moment can be the stillness that reminds you of the constant presence of God. Our everyday, ordinary lives are holy offerings to God.

When we think about being "more holy" or practicing the presence of God in our lives, we can easily make the mistake of thinking that we have to add things into our lives. But being open to the presence of God in our lives simply means that we are awake and alive to God in all the people and activities around us. If we are under the pressure to do more and more to be holier and holier, I doubt that we'll be holier! Instead I believe God wants us to see our "everyday, ordinary lives" differently, colored with the beauty of God's presence in the faces of those we love and who are strangers and even enemies; in the intricacies and mysteries of birds, animals, and plants; in the activities of our daily lives.

Brian McClaren calls this "faithing our practices" instead of just practicing our faith with more and more separate things we do. Instead we imbue our daily activities "with meaning derived from faith."[9]

So while we practice the faith with prayer and Bible study, we also practice seeing God in our daily activities and all—nature, people, encounters—that we come in contact with become a way of seeing God.

[8] Carrie Newcomer, "Holy as a Day Is Spent," from the album "The Gathering of Spirits" (Philo, 2002).
[9] Brian D. McClaren, *Finding Our Way Again: The Return of the Ancient Practices* (Thomas Nelson, 2008); p. 184.

My Reflections

How does seeing each day as holy change your perspective?

What are some daily reminders of the holy in your life?

What activities in your life can be "imbued with God" so that they put you in closer touch with God's presence in your life?

How might your daily chores, which are tedious, be "imbued with the presence of God"?

Week

2

Called:
Our Annunciation

Called

Challenge for Week 2

What image or picture would you use to remind yourself that God is calling you? This week, choose or create a meaningful image to portray your calling. Place this somewhere you will see daily and remember your calling as God's beloved.

Week Two
Called:
Our Annunciation

On a trip to Mozambique a few years ago, I was excited to discover that Nelson Mandela, the former president of South Africa and a Nobel Peace Prize winner, and his wife, Graça Machel, were coming to dinner! Of course there were at least a hundred people at the dinner I was attending that night, but nevertheless, it was a thrill to see, meet, and hear from them.

While it was initially Nelson Mandela who we were all thrilled to see, it turned out to be his wife, Graça Machel, who astonished us all! She is the widow of a former president of Mozambique who brought independence to the country, and a woman of influence in her own right as a former minister of education in the country.

Since it was a United Methodist gathering, she was the one asked to speak. She began by saying, "I am standing here as a Methodist child." She told how she was the youngest of six daughters and raised by her widowed mother who "did the impossible to educate all of us." Her father before he died made her mother and sisters vow that they would be sure that she was educated. Her mother kept her promise, but as the school was miles away, she was reluctant to let her go.

Graça told about a teacher named Mabel at the school who did everything she could to make sure that Graça had scholarships and could stay in school. Mabel, too, "did the impossible" to make sure that Graça had a good education.

Much later in her life she became the minister of education for Mozambique, following its war of independence. She was the first woman to hold the post, and she resolved to change a country that had a 93% illiteracy rate. And she followed through on that hope—five years later, the country had a 10% illiteracy rate. Graça "did the impossible" to make sure that others had an education.

She reflected on the fact that when others had "done the impossible" and gifted her with an education, then she knew that she needed to give back to others what had been given to her. If others could "do the impossible," then she too could give back the same effort and opportunity of an education for those who wouldn't otherwise have one.

As she spoke, I couldn't help but think about how many people in our culture struggle to figure out what their "purpose-driven life" is. What meaningful thing can I do with myself? What do I want to do? Instead, Graça Machel revealed to me what a purpose-*given* life is. Her purpose was given to her when she was blessed with an education. Her father, mother, sisters, teacher, and others called her to this purpose-given life and she responded by using the natural and cultivated gifts that she possessed to make it an offering to the people of her country; a people sorely in need of an education.

We all have a purpose-given life if we look to see how it is that God has called and gifted us so that we can share who we are with others and make a difference in the world around us.

This week we'll reflect upon the ways in which God has called us and how we share our gifts with others.

Day

Mary's Faithful Heart

Who You Are, What You Have, and What You Can Do

The angel said to her, "The Holy Spirit will come upon you, and the power of the Most High will overshadow you; therefore the child to be born will be holy; he will be called Son of God. . . . For nothing will be impossible with God." (Luke 1:35, 37)

The angel Gabriel's announcement (or "Annunciation") told Mary who she was (beloved and blessed by God), what she had (God's presence and goodness with her), and what she could do (anything)! One of the reasons I like Mary so much is that she had questions about what was going on around her and happening to her. She asked the angel Gabriel how it could be that she would bear the Christ into the world. The angel assured her that the Holy Spirit would come over her and that "nothing will be impossible with God" (Luke 1:37). Like Graça Machel, others "did the impossible" to gift Mary's life with what she needed.

God's calling in our lives counteracts the many messages that we receive every day from others, from advertising, from all kinds of sources that tell us who we're *not*, what we *don't* have, and what we *can't* do. Nothing could be more damaging to our souls than to listen to those messages, day after day, without some kind of antidote. The antidote is God's calling, which reminds us who we *are*, what we *do* have, and what we *can* do.

We are the beloved of God, we have God's presence and goodness in our lives, and we can do "all things through Christ who strengthens" us (Philippians 4:13, NKJV™). When we're uncertain, when we're afraid, when we're being stretched emotionally, intellectually, and spiritually, we are vulnerable to the messages of who we're not, what don't have, and what we can't do.

Pray this prayer and remember who you are, what you have, and what you can do!

O loving and gracious God,
Help me to remember who I am instead of thinking about who I'm not.
You call me by name, _____.
I am your child, loved by you,
Created in your image,
Given the free will to do all the good I can
Because you have done the impossible for me:
Made me one with you,
Given me purpose and a calling,
Gifted me with what I need to be and do.
Help me live and enjoy my best self!
Silent prayer.

Help me to remember what I have instead of thinking about
what I don't have:
I have life itself, a gift from you each day;
I have the love of friends and family whom I now call by
name;
I have a sense of purpose in life
That gives to me the calling to do the impossible for others
Whom I call by name.
Silent prayer.

Help me to remember what I can do instead of what I can't do.
Help me not to be afraid to fully live
And to believe that I can make a difference in this world.
Help me to remember that when I work with others,
We can do what none of us can do alone:
To bring peace with justice,
To eliminate as well as alleviate poverty,
And to bring freedom and joy to those who are overburdened.

As Mary said, "You have done great things for me!"
Thank you for giving generously to
Who I am, what I have, and what I can do for others.
Amen.

My Reflections

Today we read two Scriptures about our ability through God: "I can do all things through Christ who strengthens me," and "Nothing will be impossible with God." In what areas do you feel weak on your own? What seems impossible for you?

List five things that you are because you are beloved by God. List five things that you have because of God's presence and goodness. List five things that you can do because of Christ.

Day

2

What We Will Be

*"See what love the Father has given us, that we should
be called children of God; and that is what we are. . . .
Beloved, we are God's children now; what we will be has
not yet been revealed." (1 John 3:1-2)*

When I was a district superintendent in Ohio, I asked all the churches in my district to have someone tell about their calling at their annual meeting. One night the pastor asked a young girl to share how she perceived that God was calling her. She was beautiful with long, naturally curly strawberry-blonde hair and a smile that went from ear to ear, even with braces on. As she stood up to speak, she had the appearance of glowing as the light reflected off her hair and her face.

She told the assembled group of adults that although she didn't know exactly what God wanted her to do with her life, she felt God was calling her in her life. She only knew that God had a claim on who she was and what she would do with her life. She wanted to live her life in such a way that she would always be open to what it was that God wanted her to be and do. Still glowing, her hair like a halo around her head, she sat down as we all dabbed the tears in our eyes.

After a moment of silence, we regained our composure, and I said the only thing that came to mind: " 'What we will be has not yet been revealed' (1 John 3:2), but then that's the case for all of us. God has called us, God is calling us, and God will still keep calling us to be who God has created us to be."

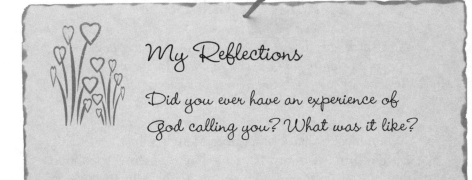

My Reflections

Did you ever have an experience of God calling you? What was it like?

Do you perceive that God keeps calling you at different times in your life?

How is God calling you at this point in your life's journey?

Day

God Calling You

"But you have God-blessed eyes—eyes that see! And
God-blessed ears—ears that hear! A lot of people,
prophets and humble believers among them, would have
given anything to see what you are seeing, to hear what
you are hearing, but never had the chance."
(*Matthew 13:16-17*, The Message)

For years I had wanted to go to Florence, Italy. It took some persuading to get my husband to go (now he's a convert to all things Italian!), but in August 2001 we spent a wonderful vacation in Florence. One of the most magical days of touring Florence and taking in its remarkable art was the day we went to San Marco's convent and museum.

San Marco is the site where the Dominican monks lived. The Dominicans were a preaching order, so it was curious to me that the famous artist, Fra Angelico, had painted frescoes in the monk's cells, depicting in each cell one aspect of Jesus' life. My imagination was captured by the idea that a monk would begin and end each day by visually meditating upon one aspect of the life that they were called to share with others through their preaching.

Room after room was filled with Jesus' birth, baptism, his teaching on the Mount, the miracles, his death and resurrection. I don't know whether a monk stayed with one aspect of the life of Jesus for the remainder of his life or if there was some plan of rotation to move the monks through the life and ministry of Jesus. (I think an effective way to learn the stories of Jesus so as to articulate them to others— whether one is a parent sharing faith with a child, a preacher with a congregation, a Sunday school teacher with a class, or someone sharing her faith with a friend—would be to study, meditate, and contemplate a visual expression of our stories of faith as well as to read them.)

But to my amazement the famous depiction of the Annunciation—when Gabriel came to Mary and announced that she was being called to bear the Christ into the world—wasn't in any one room. Instead it was at the top of the stairs to the floor where the monks lived. As people came up the stairs and rounded a corner, there in front of them was the impressive calling of Mary!

It was almost as if every day, especially at the end of the day when they'd be returning to their rooms, they needed to be reminded that God was calling them: *you are my beloved and I am with you*, the message given to Mary. It must have also served as a reminder of their calling to bear the message of Christ to the world.

I decided that I needed a daily, constant reminder of my calling, too, as I was struggling with the next steps or stage of my own life. So I downloaded a copy of Fra Angelico's *Annunciation* on my computer as the desktop picture that appears every time I turn it on. There it is: God calling Sally.

My Reflections

What image or picture would you use to remind yourself that God calls you every day to be and do what God wants you to be and do?

Consider ways to incorporate this image into your daily life. I used an image on my computer screen, you may hang one on the refrigerator or your bathroom mirror.

Day

4

Living Out Our Purpose

"But you are the ones chosen by God, chosen for the high
calling of priestly work, chosen to be a holy people, God's
instruments to do his work and speak out for him, to tell
others of the night-and-day difference he made for you—
from nothing to something, from rejected to accepted."
(1 Peter 2:9-10, The Message)

Some people make a distinction between the general purpose of our lives and a specific calling. Our purpose is the overall story of our lives, and the calling is more akin to specific tasks that fulfill the purpose of our lives. Some of us know our purpose and our calling very early and very clearly; nothing deviates from it. Others struggle more with their purpose and/or calling. We might also be under the impression that we have one thing we're meant to do in life.

I believe that our purpose is, as we discovered in Week 1, that we are beloved by God as a child of God; but our calling in how we live that out may vary and even change.

Preacher and author Barbara Brown Taylor tells the story of how, when she went to seminary, she was surrounded by people who seemed to know exactly what their calling was. They were clear that they were going to be the pastor of a local church, and most of them expected to do that for their whole working lives. Therefore they proceeded without looking right or left to fulfill that calling. Taylor wasn't quite as clear that she was called to be a pastor of a local church, much less for her whole life. Since her calling seemed somewhat different than those around her, and less clear, it filled her with self-doubt.

She began to pray earnestly (and in unusual places, like the fire escape of the building where she lived) for clarity about her calling. Then one night she had her answer, coming to her as clearly as if a voice was speaking to her. She knew then what it was that she was to do with her life; what her calling was:

> Then one night when my whole heart was open to hearing from God what I was supposed to do with my life, God said, "Anything that pleases you."
> "What?" I said, resorting to words again. "What kind of an answer is that?"
> "Do anything that pleases you," the voice in my head said again, "and belong to me."[1]

This answer from God freed her up to realize that there isn't just one right answer to the purpose of one's life, at least not hers! She did come to realize that she could live a purposeful life no matter what she did, and that freed her to combine both her sense of what "pleased" her with "belonging to God."

Barbara Brown Taylor recognizes that a *purpose* in life is to serve God, but a *calling* throughout life may change with different opportunities, experiences, and even emotional responses to life. A calling isn't a job or even a career, but the particular way in which we are living out our purpose as a beloved child of God on this earth, in this time, in whoever we are!

Taylor claims to have had seventeen different jobs in her life, including being the pastor of a local church and (currently) a college professor. All of her "jobs" have been with the purpose of belonging to God but living it out in different ways.

> Whatever I decided to do for a living, it was not *what* I did but *how* I did it that mattered. God had suggested an overall purpose, but was not going to supply the particulars for me. If I wanted a life of meaning, then I was going to have to apply the purpose for myself.[2]

She expresses what we sometimes call the "priesthood of all believers" or "ministry of all Christians." Whatever we do, we do in a way that is pleasing to God and ourselves. We make whatever our life's task is—washing dishes, delivering mail, catering, being a lawyer, selling shoes, creating websites, raising our children, caring for our frail parents—a way to live out our faith. It's ministry—serving God and our neighbor.

[1] Barbara Brown Taylor, *An Altar in the World: A Geography of Faith* (Harper-Collins, 2009); p. 110.
[2] Taylor; p. 110.

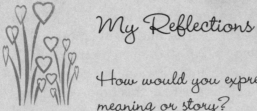

My Reflections

How would you express your life's meaning or story?

What is your calling?

How is it that whatever you do, you are doing to serve God and others?

What if the last person you encountered, who obviously was having a bad day doing whatever he or she does, had this attitude instead: I am serving God and my neighbor through this work! What difference might it have had in your encounter with him or her?

Likewise, when you're having a bad day, what would it be like if you remembered your calling?

Day

5

Uniquely You

"Take my yoke upon you, and learn from me; for I am
gentle and humble in heart, and you will find rest for
your souls. For my yoke is easy, and my burden is light."
(Matthew 11:29-30)

hree separate and unrelated quotations call to mind
that God calls us to be uniquely who we are in order
to uniquely live out our lives in belonging to God.

There's an old Jewish saying: Rabbi Zusya, when he was
an old man, said, "In the coming world, they will not ask
me: 'Why were you not Moses?' They'll ask me: 'Why
were you not Zusya?' "

We look around at other people and see their talents and gifts,
accomplishments, and opportunities and may be tempted to
try to be like them, to even *be* them. Yet God doesn't want us
to be like others, except to be like Christ. God wants us to be
truly, uniquely ourselves because God values the diversity of

talents and gifts, people and perspectives. Without our unique being, something will be missing in any given situation in which we find ourselves. We should constantly be asking ourselves—especially when we feel like we don't see things like others do or have the same gifts and abilities—how God would expect us to add to or influence a situation. God doesn't need more than one Moses, likewise God doesn't need more than one of anyone else; God needs each one of us!

> Something's your vocation [or calling] if it keeps making more of you.[3]
>
> —Gail Godwin

When we're truly and uniquely being who God has created, called, gifted, and empowered us to be, it will "make more" of us, not less. By "making more" I believe that means that it is something that doesn't diminish us but magnifies our own sense of self and relationship with God and others. When Jesus said that the yoke is easy and the burden is light, I believe he meant that when we're truly being ourselves in service to God, it may require a lot of physical, emotional, and spiritual energy, but it will also "fit." And not just "fit," but make more of us in terms of joy and satisfaction at what we're able to do. Like the image of the yoke suggests, usually what makes "more" of us, what multiplies and builds upon who we are, will be as the result of others pulling in the same direction, working together with us, and exponentially making our lives full of joy, like a cup running over.

> True vocation joins self and service when "the place where your deep gladness and the world's deep hunger meet."[4]
>
> —Frederick Buechner

What we are most passionate about is the place where we can team up with God to make a difference in the lives of others and do what we love the most all at the same time! I know a couple that loves bicycles. They find old, beat up bikes; they fix them up and then find the person who needs them most. Their deep gladness in working with bicycles has created a whole ministry of providing bicycles to kids who can't afford them, to the homeless who need them to get from shelter to shelter, and to the working poor who can't afford either a car or a bike.

Another woman I heard about made elaborate cake dolls for all the girls in her church's Sunday school program for their birthdays. As a result, the girls' attitudes changed, and they became open and receptive to her suggestions to serve others as a group and even to share with her some of their deepest hurts. These two examples represent many people who have a great passion for something in life and have been able to transform that passion into a way of reaching out to someone else.

[3] Gail Godwin, *Evensong* (Ballantine, 2000); p. 12.
[4] Frederick Buechner, *Wishful Thinking: A Seeker's ABC* (HarperSanFrancisco, 1993); p. 119.

My Reflections

Which one of these three quotations strikes you the most in your life journey at this point?

Which one of these three quotations challenges you the most?

What passion do you have that could be transformed into a ministry?

Day

6

Who Will You Be?

"So, chosen by God for this new life of love, dress in the
wardrobe God picked out for you: compassion,
kindness, humility, quiet strength, discipline.
Be even-tempered, content with second place, quick to
forgive an offense. Forgive as quickly and completely as
the Master forgave you. And regardless of what else you
put on, wear love. It's your basic, all-purpose garment.
Never be without it."
(Colossians 3:12-14, The Message)

There are so many talented musicians, artists, and authors in Minnesota, where I live. One of them, Barbara McAfee, used to work in corporate America and then discovered that her skills in organizational behavior were best utilized when she added her gift of singing and writing music. She has found that somehow people who are resistant to hearing how they might need to change are opened up through song.

Also a motivational speaker, she often performs at events a song entitled "Who You Gonna Be While You Do What You

Do?" The entire song is written in response to the question the title asks, but she goes on:

> How are you going to show up while you're passing through?
> I'm living into this question; you can, too.[5]

McAfee's words inspire me to consider my everyday interactions with people and my response to adversity as opportunities to discover my deepest gifts. Doing what we do daily can reveal our true selves.

The Colossians passage above reminds us that when we "do what we do" we might have all the "right" external things going on, like the right clothes, academic degrees, and positions of authority, but who we are in the midst of what we do is what matters the most, not only to God, but to those with whom we live and work.

As a parent, who we are with our children teaches them more about what's important to us and of value in life than all the lessons we can dutifully instruct and heap upon them. They watch us as parents and can detect whether what we're doing is consistent with what we say we value.

As a co-worker or supervisor, who we are in the midst of doing hard work or making difficult decisions can make a big difference in how people not only view our work but respect us. McAfee emphasizes throughout the song that it doesn't matter if we do a good thing if, while doing it, we "act like a jerk." Too often we don't value the means to the end in our life's work enough and we send a mixed message about our intentions and our outcomes.

No matter what we do in life, we express who we are through our life's work. Sometimes we don't have too much choice over what we do in life, but we always have a choice about who we're going to be while we do it.

[5] Barbara McAfee; http://www.barbaramcafee.com.

My Reflections

What would you call your life's work?

If we are defined by how we spend the majority of our time and how we treat others, how would you characterize your life? How would those who encounter you the most characterize your life?

Week

3

Holy:
Practicing Healthy
Habits

Holy

Challenge for Week 3

Take time this week to practice a holy, healthy habit. This might be practicing a breath prayer while taking a walk in your neighborhood. Or you might work on balancing your Spiritual Pyramid in one or more areas this week, setting short- and long-term goals for yourself.

Week Three
Holy:
Practicing Healthy Habits

Someday I would hope that people will say that the mark of my ministry was to encourage, model, and teach holy, healthy habits. It's an emphasis that has developed more recently in my ministry. I would never have considered myself to have holy, healthy habits for many years in ministry. I didn't have regular times of prayer. I didn't have disciplined ways of reading the Scriptures even though I taught up to three different Bible studies a week. I didn't read Scripture just for my soul.

Furthermore, I didn't exercise regularly, walking whenever I could was about as close as I got. I've always eaten fairly healthfully but not with intentionality.

When I became a district superintendent and didn't serve one local church as I had for 18 years prior, that's when I discovered the importance of holy, healthy habits. For one thing, I knew that I needed to tend my soul in a disciplined way because I wasn't a part of one congregation engaged in intentional discipleship.

What's more, my soul was under the stress and strain of administration, having to have difficult but crucial conversations that were hard on the heart and mind; I needed some outlet for stress and anxiety.

Driving miles every day to get to local churches or meetings made me far more sedentary than I had ever been. In a local church I could get a good mile or two of walking just by visiting someone in the hospital! Eating meals in restaurants is never as healthy as cooking at home; and increasingly I would find myself meeting someone at a restaurant for breakfast, then another person for lunch, and yet another for supper!

Then within months of becoming a district superintendent, my husband got cancer, had surgery, and there was the added concern that cancer brings. But actually it was my husband's cancer surgery that got me started on regular exercise. A month after his surgery, he wanted to go for a run around the neighborhood. He had just gotten all those tubes out! I couldn't let him go out there alone, so I went with him for about a 15-minute run . . . and I've never stopped! It has become a regular, essential part of my life ever since.

We began to eat more healthfully, counting the number of fresh fruits and vegetables that we eat each day. People thought we were on a diet, but I always told them that if you're eating the fresh fruit and vegetables that you're supposed to eat, you'll eat regularly (otherwise you can't get them all in) and you won't eat as much of the stuff you shouldn't be eating.

I began to use several different guides to prayer, which incorporate Scripture, prayers, and thought-starters. One of these guides uses the Psalms almost exclusively, and I discovered a whole new language for prayer and an appreciation for the Psalms that I had never had before. I began to read through the Bible each year and journaling one page after each day's reading. Journaling in this way revealed thoughts I didn't know I had—or maybe wouldn't have taken the time to bring to mind—and also to remember what I read as I reflected on it.

A doctor recommended that I start resistance training. I wasn't too thrilled with the thought and it's still not my favorite thing to do, but shortly after the recommendation, a new 24-hour fitness center opened about 1 ½ miles from my house. Several times a week when I'm home I run up to the center, work out, and run home again.

I received an MP3 player soon after becoming a bishop, and that has become a medium of practicing holy, healthy habits. I listen to books on tape, that I wouldn't otherwise have the time to read with my eyes, or podcasts that are stimulating to me intellectually and spiritually. Logging in 5–6 hours of running or working out each week allows me at least that much reading through my ears.

I often say that I live my life between 5 and 8 A.M. In other words, that's the time I devote to my holy, healthy habits (with the exception of trying to eat healthfully, which I try to do all day!). I'm an early bird, not a night owl, so that's what works for me. What's important is that everyone finds the rhythm that works for him or her.

These are my holy, healthy habits. I don't think we share our holy, healthy habits with each other enough; as a result we don't get ideas from each other about how to incorporate them into our lives. Each of us needs to find a rhythm of practicing our holy, healthy habits, depending upon the circumstances of our lives. Circumstances of life will get in the way from time to time, but far less so if we carve out the rhythm that works for us.

Day

1

Mary's Faithful Heart

Pondering

Now every year his parents went to Jerusalem for the festival of the Passover. And when [Jesus] was twelve years old, they went up as usual for the festival. When the festival was ended and they started to return, the boy Jesus stayed behind in Jerusalem, but his parents did not know it. Assuming that he was in the group of travelers, they went a day's journey. Then they started to look for him among their relatives and friends. When they did not find him, they returned to Jerusalem to search for him. After three days they found him in the temple, sitting among the teachers, listening to them and asking them questions. And all who heard him were amazed at his understanding and his answers. When his parents saw him they were astonished; and his mother said to him, "Child, why have you treated us like this? Look, your father and I have been searching for you in great anxiety." He said to them, "Why were you searching for me? Did you not know that I must be in my Father's house?" But they did not understand what he said to them. Then he went down with them and came to Nazareth, and was obedient to them. His mother treasured all these things in her heart. (Luke 2:41-51)

*M*ary was a ponderer. It's not hard to imagine that she pondered just what bearing the Christ child into the world would mean for her and the child. Later, she pondered the events of Jesus' birth with the coming of the shepherds and the singing of the angels (Luke 2:19). When she and Joseph presented Jesus in the Temple (Luke 2:22-38), Simeon told her that her child was destined for great things which would also involve suffering, including her own. Surely she must have pondered, "What child is this?" And then when her young son told her and Joseph that he needed to be in his Father's house, she pondered all these events (Luke 2:41-51). As recorded several times in the Bible, Mary pondered these things in her heart.

To *ponder* means to think deeply, contemplate, or meditate. Holy, healthy habits are meant to help us ponder our lives in light of the story of our faith, what God is saying and doing through us, to lead an examined life in light of the Spirit. Too often we read Scripture as quickly as we can without thinking deeply about what it means in our lives, or we rattle off our prayers instead of seeking to draw to mind and heart and articulating what is deepest in our hearts—our hurts and our joys.

Ponder Mary's own story for a minute. Reread Luke 2:41-51 (see previous page), and consider the reflection questions that follow.

My Reflections

When you read the passage, ask yourself the following questions:

How am I like Mary in this story?

How have I "lost" Jesus in my life?

Where might I "find" Jesus in my life?

What don't I understand about Jesus in my life?

What could God be saying to me through this passage?

Day

2

Prayer Beads

"Do not worry about anything, but in everything by prayer and supplication with thanksgiving let your requests be made known to God. And the peace of God, which surpasses all understanding, will guard your hearts and your minds in Christ Jesus."
(Philippians 4:6-7)

My prayer life was totally revolutionized when a Norwegian friend taught me about prayer beads.[1] Essentially, it is a circle of beads with meaning assigned to each one. Holding the circle of beads around my hand and keeping one bead at a time between my thumb and forefingers helps me to focus my prayer life.

Prayer beads are not jewelry but an aid to prayer. Unlike a bracelet, prayer beads should just slip over the fingers so that they circle the outer hand and palm. The beads and what they represent are as follows:

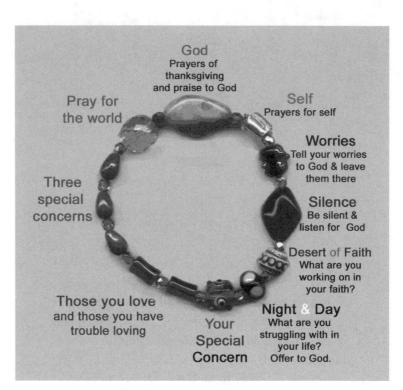

Big Gold Bead: God
  Offer prayers of thanksgiving and praise to God.
Silvery or Clear Bead: Self
  Say prayers for yourself.
Bumpy or Triangular Bead: Worries
  Tell all your worries to God and leave them there.
Light Blue Bead: Silence
  Be silent and listen for God.
Wooden Bead: Desert of Faith
  What are you working on in your faith?
Clear with Black Bead: Night and Day
  What are you struggling with in your life? Offer it
  to God.

Green Bead: Your Special Concern
Pray about the most pressing or important concern to you personally.
2 Red Beads: People to Love
Pray for those you love and those you have trouble loving.
3 Purple Beads: Additional Concerns
Lift up three additional concerns.
Deep Blue or Turquoise Bead: The World
Pray for world concerns.

As your mind wanders (or is it just mine?), holding the beads in your hand guides you back to your prayers instead of starting over or giving up!

The beads can be adapted, but I find that this general structure helps me to pray more inclusively for the world, for others, and for myself as well as to give thanks and praise to God. I encourage using them; and if they prove helpful in prayer, find the right beads for each of the representations. I hope it revolutionizes your prayer life as much as it has mine.

---

[1] Sally Dyck, "Prayer Beads as Teaching Tools," in *Becoming A Praying Congregation: Churchwide Leadership Tools*, with Rueben P. Job (Abingdon Press, 2009); pp. 156–159.

My Reflections

If you have prayer beads, use them now and write out your prayers as you come to each bead. If not, use the picture of prayer beads on p. 76 as a reference as you write out your prayer.

How does adding this structure to your prayers differ from when you pray without beads? Do you find your prayers more focused?

Day

3

The Spiritual Pyramid

"One final word, friends. We ask you—urge is more like it—that you keep on doing what we told you to do to please God, not in a dogged religious plod, but in a living, spirited dance. You know the guidelines we laid out for you from the Master Jesus. God wants you to live a pure life. . . . Learn to appreciate and give dignity to your body, not abusing it, as is so common among those who know nothing of God. . . . God hasn't invited us into a disorderly, unkempt life but into something holy and beautiful—as beautiful on the inside as the outside."
(1 Thessalonians 4:1-2, 4-5, 7, The Message)

Holy, healthy habits entail not only practices but some degree of regularity and balance. Too often we find ourselves spiritually depleted even though we have been engaged in one aspect of what we might call a spiritual life. For women it seems that service can take over our time and efforts and we forget to nurture our souls. For others it may be that there's no regular worship or Bible study, and so an annual retreat is the sole source of spiritual nourishment.

As I've observed and listened to people over the years, I've reflected on the need for a well-balanced spiritual diet. So, I developed what I call The Spiritual Pyramid.

The Spiritual Pyramid

A Guide to Holy Choices
Recommended by Bishop Sally Dyck

Retreats
8 to 16 hours per year

Worship
1 to 2 hours per week

Service and Outreach
30 to 90 minutes per month

Small-Group Discipleship
2 hours per week

Service in the Church
1 to 2 hours per week

Bible Study and Prayer
30 minutes per day

Photos clockwise from top: © 2004 Minnesota Annual Conference; UMNS photo by Carol Kreamer; UMNS photo by John Gordon; public domain; GBOD photo; UMNS photo by Tim Tanton

The Spiritual Pyramid is based on personal Bible study and prayer. Our personal devotions or time with God are like what water and air are to our bodies; they're essential for a healthy body. Meeting with others in small groups builds upon our personal devotions as well as service in the church, corporate worship, and service to our communities. While there are suggested amounts of time for each one, what's most important is that we see the proportion of each time period in relation to the amount in any one that we are spending. If all our time is in service to the church, such as teaching Sunday school, and we're not engaged in our own personal devotions, small group, or worship at all, we shouldn't be surprised if we find ourselves spiritually depleted. At the top of the Pyramid is a retreat. I've found some people who rely only on an annual retreat to nourish them, and it's almost as if their Spiritual Pyramid is upside down! The Spiritual Pyramid revealed to me that one of the areas I have difficulty keeping in balance is hands-on outreach to a community. Therefore, I look for opportunities, even if they're irregular, to engage in reaching out to alleviate suffering, such as serving a meal at a homeless shelter.

None of us has a perfectly balanced spiritual life. The Spiritual Pyramid isn't meant to make us feel bad about an area that is neglected; rather it helps us be intentional about finding ways to increase in that area for the overall welfare of our spirits.

My Reflections

How would you designate your time (be generous in the amounts, including attending church or small group, spending time with people before and afterward, etc.) spent in each of these areas?

Is there an area that dominates the whole Pyramid?

Is there an area that seems to be neglected?

What one thing could you do to balance out your spiritual life?

Remember: The point is _balance_, not adding more hours. A balancing of these areas of the spiritual life will help us be spiritually strong and healthy, especially as we face the stresses and strains of life.

Day

4

Scripture in Our Hearts

*"Hear, O Israel: The LORD our God, the LORD is one.
Love the LORD your God with all your heart and with all
your soul and with all your strength. These commandments that I give you today are to be upon your hearts."
(Deuteronomy 6:4-6, NIV)*

There's a story from the Jewish tradition that I reflect on over and over. A rabbi told his people that they needed to study the Torah, or Scriptures, so that the Scriptures would be *on* their hearts. One of his students asked him, "Why *on* our hearts and not *in* our hearts?" The rabbi answered, "Only God can put Scripture *in* our hearts. But reading the sacred text can put them *on* our hearts so that when our hearts are broken, the holy words will fall inside."

Mary's pondering opened her heart to let God's words fall into it as she watched her own life and the life, ministry, death, and resurrection of her son.

As a preacher and teacher of the Bible over the years, I have seen with my own eyes how people—and this includes me—can hear certain Scriptures over and over again, but when something happens in our lives, it's as if that Scripture "falls inside" our hearts. Something happens in our lives that makes a passage seem so real, comforting, challenging, the perfect description of our experience.

I know a young woman who is entering the ministry. She's young and when a team of people met with her, they questioned whether she had enough life experience to be in ministry. She recalled a host of bad things that had happened in her family, including bankruptcy through which they lost a business and home. Her faith helped her cope with these difficulties in her teenage years. Then after college, she was working in a building where a gunman opened fire and terrorized the workers. She and her co-workers spent five hours on the floor of a closet, not yards from the front door of the building, unable to move for fear that he would see them and kill them. She told the team that was interviewing her about this experience and said, "When you're in a situation like that, you know what it means that God loves you and that's what really matters." All those Scriptures "fell" into her heart that day.

Pondering leads to practicing or living. The Scripture becomes a part of who we are; it's our story now that our heart has been broken and the Word has fallen into it. So no longer do we "mouth" a passage, but we "live" it; it becomes the living Word through us.

My Reflections

What are your practices in reading Scripture? What do you read and when?

Do you like to read Scripture? If not, what gets in the way?

Has a particular Scripture or Bible passage ever "fallen into" your heart because of an experience in your life? If so, which Scripture and what life experience?

Day

5

Preparing for the Marathons of Life

*"Everyone then who hears these words of mine and acts
on them will be like a wise man who built his house on
rock. The rain fell, the floods came, and the winds blew
and beat on that house, but it did not fall, because it had
been founded on rock. And everyone who hears these
words of mine and does not act on them will be like a
foolish man who built his house on sand. The rain fell,
and the floods came, and the winds blew and beat against
that house, and it fell—and great was its fall!"*
(Matthew 7:24-27)

A while ago, I lived in a neighborhood where Olympic
award-winning swimmer Diana Munz also lived. The
summer before the 2004 Olympics, a friend of mine who
worked for the local public radio station interviewed her. In
the interview, Diana described how she was preparing for
the Olympics. Throughout the year, every decision she
made—when to get out of bed, whether to continue in college, how much time to spend with friends—was made in
light of the Olympics. Every choice could determine her
readiness to win a gold medal.

She trained 7 days a week, 3 times a day with no exceptions even for holidays. There was no time or room in her life for anything other than practice, practice, practice. Diana said that the Olympics don't just take place every four years; they take place every day, often before dawn. In other words, you don't just show up for the Olympics without having prepared, but every choice you make prior to the start of the race will work toward determining its outcome. And many of those choices are made "before dawn."

Some days I feel like I'm in the Olympics, or at least a marathon, as I face work, demands, pressing deadlines, and exacting details which make for long and exhausting days. We all seek to balance pressures, especially as women, who also often do a "second shift" when we get home with housework, cooking, and child-rearing. In addition, we care for ailing parents, teach Sunday school, and hope to be our best selves.

How do we do it?

We have to show up well prepared in body, mind, and spirit. None of us is probably ever as well prepared and practiced as an Olympic award-winner, but unless we do spiritual, mental, and physical "strength training," it's pretty hard to face the marathons of our lives.

My Reflections

In what area of your life do you need "strength training"? Physically, mentally, spiritually, and even emotionally?

What's one thing you could do to better care for yourself as you face the "marathon" of your life?

Day

6

Breathing in God's Presence

"Rejoice always, pray without ceasing, give thanks in all circumstances; for this is the will of God in Christ Jesus for you." (1 Thessalonians 5:16-18)

I once knew a couple in a church that I served, one of whom had a mother who was coming to the end of her life. She had made the choice months before not to receive further treatment and now the time had come when death was near. I didn't know her that well, but when she began to face the end, the family called for me to visit her.

Her main concern was that she could not pray. She wondered if I could help her to pray. Not just pray *for* her, but *teach* her to pray. Not knowing her very well, I asked her how she normally prayed. She told me that in the past she would simply give thanks to God: for life, for every good thing, for the beauty of the day, for her loved ones, whatever came to mind. Her daughter told me later that her mother would stop and thank God for the smallest of things, such as being able to thread the needle on the sewing machine after her macular degeneration made the task nearly impossible.

But now it was very upsetting for her because, as she put it, she could no longer pray. I asked her if she found it difficult to thank God when she was in this situation of facing death, of experiencing pain (which she had the night before), and when she was afraid. She said that it was, but she said it such a way that it didn't seem like this was the root of the problem.

Recognizing that most of her prayer had been in the form of thanksgiving, I told her that it was okay to ask God for help. She looked at me in amazement and asked, "Is it okay to ask for help? Is that a prayer?" I assured her that it was and that all she needed to say was, "Help me, Jesus."

She responded, "That's what I was praying last night: 'Help me, O Lord, help me!' And that's a prayer?" I assured her that it was and thought about how for many of us that's the *only* kind of prayer we say!

But I went a step further, realizing that soon even speaking words would become difficult for her. She was always hooked up to oxygen and felt very dependent upon it. I told her to imagine that "just as that oxygen goes into your body, you are also breathing in God's presence and peace. That's a prayer, too."

"That's a prayer?" she asked again. "Oh, I like that!"

After she died, I was informed that she told everyone that she was breathing in God's presence and peace as she breathed in her oxygen. As she breathed in oxygen, she breathed in God . . . and as long as she had breath, she was constantly praying.

Breath prayer has been a common form of prayer since ancient times. The Hebrew word *ruach* means "wind" or "breath" as well as "spirit" and reminds us that praying is or can be as natural as breathing. Short phrases from the Psalms; phrases like "help me, Jesus" or "thank you, Jesus"; or other meaningful phrases are prayed as one breathes in and out. Breath prayer is to have on our lips what we have on our hearts. Breath prayer can be a way of calming our spirits, focusing our hearts and minds, and it may also be a way to pray our way into a comforting sleep.

My Reflections

What's your most common form of prayer? Giving thanks, asking for help, or what?

What phrase would you use for a breath prayer?

When might you use breath prayer?

Week

4

Equipped:
A Community of Faith

Challenge for Week 4

Consider how you have experienced true community throughout different times in your life. How can you, likewise, offer true community to others? Look for opportunities this week to extend an invitation to someone who might be hungry for community.

Week Four
Equipped:
A Community of Faith

Every child with a piece of paper and a pair of scissors quickly learns that every snowflake is different, whether it's the one created with paper or the one that falls from the sky. A scientific description of snowflakes reveals that they form when water vapor condenses into a crystal.

But each snowflake is literally a work of art, whose creation makes each one different. If snowflakes are a work of art, then the wind is the artist because the wind bounces the flake from one temperature to another, from one level of humidity to another, from one condition to another, until it changes and grows. No two snowflakes can ever possibly follow the same path or encounter even the same conditions in the same way, so no two snowflakes are alike. But all snowflakes have something in common: they all share at their core a 6-sided symmetry.

Like the core 6-sided symmetry of a snowflake, we all have the core of our faith in Jesus Christ, which leads us to God. If we are like the snowflakes, God is like the wind, sending us each on different journeys in life to understand different aspects of the world around us and who God is, journeys that make us who we are.

I read a quote once, attributed to Vesta Kelly: "Snowflakes are one of nature's most fragile things, but just look what they can do when they stick together."

Sometimes it snows and the conditions keep the flakes from sticking together. Nothing much happens in a snowstorm if the snowflakes are isolated, floating entities in the sky, staying uniquely alone. It's when the conditions allow them to come together, one flake with another, that the landscape is changed into a wintry wonderland, sidewalks and streets require work, and occasionally we get a snow day!

We are all uniquely created by God—a work of art ourselves! We all have our own unique experiences and expressions of faith due to the events and conditions of our own lives. We could all live in our uniqueness as followers of Jesus; but when we all stay uniquely alone, lots of things don't happen in our lives, our community, and our world.

When we experience illness or death, being uniquely alone isn't very comforting. When we have questions of faith, our minds keep whirling through our own thoughts unless we have others to guide us through them as they've wrestled with the same questions. When we see suffering all around us and throughout the world, we're fully aware that we as individuals can't make a big difference; but together as a community of faith, we can make a significant difference.

Yet increasingly, according to surveys and studies, more and more people decide that they can be Christian without a community of disciples around them. While Jean-Paul Sartre is often described as an atheist, it seems to me that many Christians have ascribed to his saying: "Hell is other people." "I love Jesus, I just don't always like all the people in my church." People don't always say it quite that bluntly, but the end result is the same. Yet in order to follow Jesus and grow spiritually, being uniquely alone won't work.

Jesus calls us into community, and sometimes it seems as if the Jesus community includes some pretty difficult people! Maybe even us! But if we are beloved children of God, then the community in which Jesus calls us to live out our faith is a beloved community. We need each other in order to become more like Christ, supported and challenged so that our uniqueness is continually under construction and even so we can better stick together!

Community of the Spirit

In those days Mary set out and went with haste to a Judean town in the hill country, where she entered the house of Zechariah and greeted Elizabeth. When Elizabeth heard Mary's greeting, the child leaped in her womb. And Elizabeth was filled with the Holy Spirit and exclaimed with a loud cry, "Blessed are you among women, and blessed is the fruit of your womb. And why has this happened to me, that the mother of my Lord comes to me? For as soon as I heard the sound of your greeting, the child in my womb leaped for joy. And blessed is she who believed that there would be a fulfillment of what was spoken to her by the Lord."
(Luke 1:39-45)

While Mary was unique in her calling to bear the Christ in the world, she didn't stay uniquely alone. No sooner did the angel Gabriel leave after delivering the message that she would bear a son than Mary "went with haste" to a nearby town. She went straight to her cousin Elizabeth's house and stayed there for three months (Luke 1:56).

Elizabeth was pregnant with John the Baptist. Together Mary and Elizabeth found strength in their uniqueness by being in a community of the Spirit. They understood what was going on in each other's body and soul. They worshiped together as they sang songs of praise to God for all the good things that God was doing in their lives. They were uniquely who they were but together in mutual support, worship, and prayer. They were in a community of the Spirit as they pondered what all these things meant in their lives.

Uniquely alone, Mary pondered; with Elizabeth she had a "small group" in which to articulate what was going on with herself and with Elizabeth. In order to grow in our faith, we need to bring our unique selves to a small group of other unique selves to help us understand the Scriptures and our lives, to learn to pray and to pray for each other, to support one another but also hold each other accountable for our practices and growth, and to have the opportunity to share with those who are going through similar experiences in life and faith.

My Reflections

What are your experiences with a small group within your faith community?

How has a small group enriched your life and faith?

What is the most critical aspect of a helpful small group?

How has a small group helped you articulate what you have pondered?

What's the challenge in being in a small group?

Day 2

Holy Conferencing

*"But speaking the truth in love, we must grow up in
every way into him who is the head, into Christ, from
whom the whole body, joined and knit together by every
ligament with which it is equipped, as each part is working properly, promotes the body's growth in building itself up in love. . . . clothe yourselves with the new self,
created according to the likeness of God in true righteousness and holiness." (Ephesians 4:15-16, 24)*

Last week I shared with you my Spiritual Pyramid
(p. 80), which I use to help maintain a balanced spiritual life. A balanced spiritual life includes both time alone
with God and together with others. Without both we become
unbalanced in our relationship with God and others.

Many of the components in the Spiritual Pyramid necessary
for a balanced spiritual life are means of grace that position

us to grow in faith and spiritual maturity, such as personal prayer, reading Scripture, and fasting. Yet other components of this balanced spiritual life involve participation and invested relationships with others. Corporate worship, participation in the Lord's Supper, and service to those in need also put us in the position of growing in our faith and spiritual maturity as we worship and serve side by side with others. John Wesley, the founder of Methodism, also considered "Christian conferencing" to be a means of grace and encouraged people to practice it in order to grow in faith and spiritual maturity.

What is "Christian conferencing," or, as it has come to be called, "holy conferencing"?

Christian or holy conferencing is the willingness to engage in "conferring" with others to discern truth and a path forward when there is disagreement and difference of opinion. For most of us today, we would rather avoid conferring with others who disagree with us. It's easier to leave the Christian table of conferencing than to stay at the table. To expect that such "conferring" or staying at the table will actually put us in the position of growing in our faith and spiritual maturity is almost impossible for us to believe.

But *how* we discourse with each other, relate to one another, and regard others who disagree with us is *as* important as the final outcome of our discernment and discussion. When we practice holy conferencing, we do grow in faith and spiritual maturity because we "lead a life worthy of the calling to which [we] have been called, with all humility and gentleness, with patience, bearing with one another in love, making every effort to maintain the unity of the Spirit in the bond of peace" (Ephesians 4:1b-3).

Wesley believed so strongly in Christian conferencing as a means of grace that he insisted that there is no such thing as solitary religion—we cannot be Christian by ourselves!

> "Holy solitaries" is a phrase no more consistent with the gospel than holy adulterers. The gospel of Christ knows of no religion, but social; no holiness but social holiness.

We are shocked to hear the phrase "holy adulterers," because we take for granted that people can be religious or spiritual without others. The spiritual surprise is that in community we can be made whole, more holy, and more Christlike.

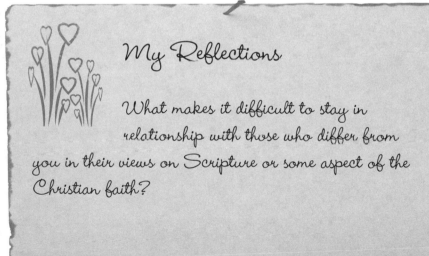

My Reflections

What makes it difficult to stay in relationship with those who differ from you in their views on Scripture or some aspect of the Christian faith?

How have you grown in faith and spiritual maturity when you stayed in relationship with those who disagreed with you about deep spiritual matters?

Day

3

An Unlikely Family

*"Therefore be imitators of God, as beloved children, and
live in love, as Christ loved us and gave himself up for
us, a fragrant offering and sacrifice to God."*
(Ephesians 5:1-2)

A community of faith puts us into relationship with people who we might not otherwise even know, much less learn to love. My life has been so enriched by the people I have met in church.

Mrs. Riley is my "other mother." Even my biological mother calls her that. My mother lives in Washington state, but I spent twenty-five years in the Cleveland, Ohio, area. For twenty of those years, Mrs. Riley was like a mother to me, and continues to be so now, even if from a distance.

She is in her mid-nineties, an African American, and the widow of a United Methodist minister. She taught first grade in Chicago and Cleveland for years after getting an education herself. While she has no immediate blood relatives who live near her in Cleveland, she has a revolving door with people in and out all day and throughout the week; so much so that at times she complains about how she gets no peace and quiet. But she loves being Grand Central Station among her friends.

Mrs. Riley needs to feed. Even at her age, she still cooks up a storm. Whatever she cooks, it's soul food—literally food to comfort body and soul. No one goes out her door without having eaten something! And, half the time, without taking some food with them!

It's at her table that people—mostly a conglomeration of women up to 40 years younger than she is—experience not only the food that she has prepared but the community that develops through the sharing of life stories, laughing and talking, getting queried about whatever is going on in the world or life, and generally being a beloved child of God.

There, I've heard the stories of what it was like to grow up as an African American in Florida in the early 1920's, where as a little girl she would have to walk by white elementary schools to go to a Methodist church where the only school for her was in the basement. I learned the stories of how when her mother died, she was sent up north to Akron, Ohio, to live with her grandparents. She married the new, young pastor at the Methodist church and began an adventure of living across the entire United States as he was sent from one place to another to shepherd the African American congregations. I learned the stories of the civil rights movement in Cleveland where Rev. Riley brought Martin Luther King, Jr., and Malcolm X into the heart of the city. I learned the stories of the coming together of the African American

Methodists with the rest of the church after being separate for so many generations.

I'd read about these events in school and on my own, but when you hear the stories at the table of the one who is feeding you and whom you love so deeply, they become a part of you in a whole different way. That's what church is at its best: we become part of one another. What one has suffered in life, we suffer together. What one has rejoiced in, we rejoice in together. What's part of one's life becomes part of ours.

Mrs. Riley's need to feed builds community, shares faith, and draws people together whose worlds might otherwise never touch. Sounds like the purpose of the church, doesn't it?

My Reflections

How has your life been enriched and your horizons expanded because of a faith community?

Who is the most unlikely person that your faith community has brought into your life? What have you learned from that person about life and faith?

How does your faith community encourage you to widen your circle of acquaintances so that your uniqueness is enhanced by others?

Day

4

True Community

Awe came upon everyone, because many wonders and signs were being done by the apostles. All who believed were together and had all things in common; they would sell their possessions and goods and distribute the proceeds to all, as any had need. Day by day, as they spent much time together in the temple, they broke bread at home and ate their food with glad and generous hearts, praising God and having the goodwill of all the people. And day by day the Lord added to their number those who were being saved. (Acts 2:43-47)

My niece is in her early thirties and often starts our conversations together with, "My biggest beef with the church is . . ." and proceeds to explain what the church *isn't* doing. She is quite frankly very disappointed in the church. She was raised in the church and caught enough of the church's message that she feels that Christians should be living differently as a result of what we profess.

When she comes to visit me, she goes to church with me. One Sunday morning we were sitting together before worship, and she was busily reading the bulletin. It was packed with all kinds of information about all that was going on at or through the church.

All of a sudden, she whispered to me, "If I lived here, I'd go to this." And she pointed to something in the bulletin. I nearly fell off the seat in my eagerness to find out just what *this* was! It was the Wednesday community meal. During our weekend visit, she had been talking about how much she was missing community. She had moved to Boston for the year to go to school and had left her community of friends in California. She was living by herself in a small apartment and missing those in her life with whom she regularly cooked, ate, and spent time. She was hungry for community.

I couldn't help but think of all the people who regularly cook, eat, and spend most of their time alone. And not just young adults like my niece, but elderly people and many others who live alone. We live uniquely alone more and more, yet desire community more and more. And true community, not just fellowship.

Fellowship smacks of long-time friends having a good time with each other. Community is open to others, new and old. There's always a place at the table for them to sit down; the tables aren't already filled. Conversation includes others; it does not just revolve around that which a newcomer wouldn't know. True community is interested in each one, especially the new person, and what new insights, experiences, and interests this person might have.

Sometimes I worry that my niece might actually go to a community dinner at a local church. Will she find true community—one that is open to getting to know her, listening to her and her interests, and accepting who she is? Or will they close themselves off, not leaving room at the table for her to sit down, not including her in the conversation, not being open to who she is and what she has to offer?

My Reflections

Have you ever experienced the desire for true community? How did you find it?

How do you purposefully extend true community to others?

Day

5

The Change You Wish to See

"Let each of you look not to your own interests, but to the interests of others. Let the same mind be in you that was in Christ Jesus." (Philippians 2:4-5)

Diana Butler Bass is an author of books like *Christianity for the Rest of Us*, which gives practical as well as theological support for those of us who are a part of a mainline denomination. On a radio interview, I heard her describe what she imagined in a church for her then 8-year-old daughter. She said, "I so want the kind of justice-oriented, prayerful, intellectually rigorous, beautiful faith [for her]. . . . I want her to be able to experience that in a way that makes sense for her as she is going to live well into the twenty-first century."[1] Bass imagines a church welcoming of her daughter and others, one that is radically inclusive, non-sexist, and deeply compassionate in its expression of Christian community. "I hope that it's there for her; I think it will be," Bass says.[2]

The only way that it will be there for her daughter is for people in the church, like Bass, to work toward this goal—to be a church that reflects this vision and this true heart desire in a faith community. Diana Butler Bass is a professional in leading and teaching about what a church can be in the twenty-first century, but it doesn't take a professional to make a difference in a local church's "justice-oriented, prayerful, intellectually rigorous, beautiful faith."

Mahatma Gandhi said, "Be the change you wish to see in the world." If we can imagine a better, more inclusive, justice-seeking, compassionate church for the future, then we need to be the change we wish to see in the church.

I once heard of a man who complained all the time about the church he went to. His friends would listen to his complaints over and over again, every Monday morning over coffee. He didn't like the "bumpety-bump-bump" music with drums and guitars. The pastor used illustrations from books and movies that he knew nothing about. He didn't like the informality of the pastor who wore blue jeans and a t-shirt for church. The list went on and on. Finally one of his friends asked him, "Why do you go to that church?" The man's eyes filled with tears and he quietly said, "Because it's the only church that my granddaughter will attend." That's truly sacrificial and what it means to pass on the faith at your own personal expense. It's what each of us needs to do in order to insure that the next generation receives the faith—just as Diana Butler Bass no longer looks for only what she needs but works for the kind of church that she wants for her daughter.

[1] Interviewed on the radio show, Interfaith Voices, aired December 21, 2006; available: http://interfaithradio.org/node/108.
[2] Interfaith Voices interview (12/21/06).

My Reflections

What kind of church do you want for your children or grandchildren—the next generation?

What can you do to help make it that way? How can you be the "change you wish to see"?

Day

6

The Poured-Out Church

Then he said to them all, "If any want to become my fol-
lowers, let them deny themselves and take up their cross
daily and follow me. For those who want to save their life
will lose it, and those who lose their life for my sake will
save it." (Luke 9:23-24)

Barbara Brown Taylor wrote a book entitled *Leaving Church* in which she describes her decision to no longer pastor a local church but to teach at a college. Part of her decision was based in the reality that the church isn't all that it can be and that's disappointing; but even in her leaving church, she acknowledges that she had the church's story in her heart:

> The church has given me the eyes with which I see, as well
> as the words with which I speak. The church has given me
> a community in which to figure out what has happened
> to me in the world. It has given me a place to love and

121

grieve, within a tradition far older and wiser than I. It is the church that has poured me into the world, in other words—which is counterintuitive. How can a church survive that keeps pouring itself into the world? I cannot possibly say. All I know is the gospel truth: those willing to give everything away are the ones with anything worth keeping; those willing to look death full in the face are the ones with the most abundant lives. Go figure. . . . Leaving church, I believe, is what church is for—leaving on a regular basis, leaving to see what God is up to in the world and joining God there.[3]

Church has shaped who Taylor is even as she no longer relates to the church in the same ways that she once did as a pastor. But church goes with her wherever she goes! The practices, the community, the teachings, and the counterintuitive messages of the gospel go with her out the door of the church and into the world where she lives, works, and relates to others.

My concern is for many people who are not a part of a faith community that pours itself out for the world, giving to others, shaping faith, connecting lives, and supporting one another. How will their lives be shaped by church unless we connect with them?

Church is more than where we go; it's who we are after we've been sent forth at the end of the service. We're called to be church for others.

[3] Barbara Brown Taylor, "The Poured-Out Church," in *Christian Century*, May 29, 2007; p. 35.

My Reflections

Do you long for a poured-out church?

Do you "leave" church like that?

How can we be church for others when we leave church at the end of the service each week?

How can you help your faith community become a poured-out church?

Week

5

Joyful:
An Evangelistic Heart

Joyful

Challenge for Week 5

Consider how your own evangelistic heart has grown and developed through the years. Who has "scattered joy" in your life? Whose contagious joy caused you to grow in your faith? If you are able, contact one of these people this week. Write a note or send an e-mail, tweet, or text. Let them know you are grateful for their evangelistic heart.

Week Five
Joyful:
An Evangelistic Heart

*W*omen are natural evangelists! What I mean is that women are quick to share with each other—with their mothers and sisters and daughters, with their best friends and even co-workers—what is deep in their hearts. Deep in their hearts can be joy and gladness; deep in their hearts can be sorrow and pain.

So when women are filled with good news, excitement, or deep interest in something, such as what God is doing in their lives, I find that women talk about it a lot! Maybe not publicly, standing in front of a large group and pontificating about their religious beliefs, but over cups of coffee, in book groups (whether the book is "religious" or not), and even in line at the grocery store.

But I doubt that many of these women who talk about their faith over coffee, in book groups, or in grocery lines would raise their hand if you asked, "Who here has an evangelistic heart?" But they might raise their hands if they understood that "evangelism" isn't preaching like Billy Graham or buttonholing someone with the question, "Have you been saved?" Evangelism means having a conversation that shares the love and grace of Jesus with others. Sometimes we use our words, and sometimes our actions speak louder than our words.

An evangelistic heart is one that is sincerely interested and excited about being a person who is on a journey of faith. Some would describe it as having a personal relationship with Jesus Christ, but others might express it as a journey with others toward God. An evangelistic heart doesn't kick anyone off the journey because they express their experience differently!

An evangelistic heart is interested in how other people experience and express their faith in God, and the best way to do that is to talk to them about it. That means the subject of God seems to come up in conversations naturally, regardless of whether or not the person goes to your church, or how well you know the person, or even if they would describe themselves as Christian. Just as it's natural to talk about the weather, which is everywhere and constantly impacting us, why wouldn't we talk about God, who is everywhere, all the time?

An evangelistic heart is also a heart that is broken. A heart that breaks is part of what happens when we journey with Jesus. An evangelistic heart breaks for the people in this world who suffer physically, emotionally, spiritually, and any other way that we can suffer. Someone with an evangelistic heart might be accused of being a "bleeding heart," and if that's the case for you just say, "Why, thank you!

That's the nicest thing anyone's said about me today!" God's heart breaks for those in need and breaks when our hearts don't seem to care. An evangelistic heart beats for the kid never picked on the team, the mothers whose children precede them in death for any reason, the homeless man on the street corner . . . the list goes on. An evangelistic heart has a passion—at least one—for people in need and does what she can to reach out.

A person with an evangelistic heart is a beautiful person . . . like you.

The Magnificat

And Mary said, "My soul magnifies the Lord, and my spirit rejoices in God my Savior, for he has looked with favor on the lowliness of his servant. Surely, from now on all generations will call me blessed; for the Mighty One has done great things for me, and holy is his name. His mercy is for those who fear him from generation to generation. He has shown strength with his arm; he has scattered the proud in the thoughts of their hearts. He has brought down the powerful from their thrones, and lifted up the lowly; he has filled the hungry with good things, and sent the rich away empty. He has helped his servant Israel, in remembrance of his mercy, according to the promise he made to our ancestors, to Abraham and to his descendants forever." (Luke 1:46-55)

*M*ary had an evangelistic heart! After the angel Gabriel left Mary, she went with haste to spend some women-time with her cousin, Elizabeth. Mary had just received the news of a lifetime, what in fact becomes the news of all time! And Elizabeth also had some good news residing in her womb. No woman is going to keep this good news to herself for long, and so upon Mary's arrival, Elizabeth and Mary both began to sing and rejoice together. I can imagine them jumping and dancing around and around, hugging each other like sisters, and laughing and crying all at the same time. Who says the Holy Spirit doesn't come upon us like that sometimes? In fact, I wonder if the Holy Spirit wants to come upon us like that more often!

Mary's song is often referred to as the *Magnificat* because it begins with the words, "My soul magnifies the Lord." Mary's heart is bursting with joy and gladness for all that God has done for her. "Tell out, my soul, the greatness of the Lord!"[1]

Joy is the hardest thing to keep to yourself. We can sit on sorrow for a long time, but joy almost can't live without expression to another person. When joy bubbles up because of what God is doing in our lives, and we share with someone else, that's an evangelistic heart at work!

[1] "Tell Out, My Soul," words by Timothy Dudley-Smith, *The United Methodist Hymnal* (The United Methodist Publishing House, 1989); p. 200.

My Reflections

Have you ever had such good news that you couldn't wait to tell your mother, sister, friend, co-worker, the woman on the bus, <u>anyone</u> because it was so wonderful? What was it, and who did you tell?

Sometimes "joy" isn't quite the word for it, but a deep interest or excitement about learning and growing in our faith causes us to connect with people—whether we know them or not—about spiritual matters. Do you talk to anyone about God in your daily life?

Day

2

Shining Through

"You are the salt of the earth; but if salt has lost its taste, how can its saltiness be restored? It is no longer good for anything, but is thrown out and trampled under foot. You are the light of the world. A city built on a hill cannot be hid. No one after lighting a lamp puts it under the bushel basket, but on the lampstand, and it gives light to all in the house. In the same way, let your light shine before others, so that they may see your good works and give glory to your Father in heaven." (Matthew 5:13-16)

Cornelia (Connie) Wieck is a United Methodist missionary serving in China where she has taught English for about ten years. Before she became a missionary, she participated in a mission intern program for three years to see what it would be like to serve in that capacity. As part of that experience, Connie taught English to junior high school students in Kyoto, Japan, through a program at the Kyoto YWCA. There, she taught environmental studies, and so the practice of English centered around how the students might care for the environment.

Connie's evangelistic heart shone through her teaching and how she related to her students. She describes an experience she had:

> In our environmental study groups, I said nothing about my religious orientation, as my goal was to introduce these young people to a service they could provide to their world and country. One day, a mother of one of the students came to me and said, "My daughter asked me why you cared so much about the world and its people. I told her it was because you were a Christian. She thought about this deeply and then said, 'I want to be just like her.' " I suddenly realized that the presence of God is always shining through us, embracing others when we (or they) least expect it. What a wonderful gift of love God has given us to share with others! This was when I began to focus on a commitment to the church through full-time missionary service. [2]

Connie's calling was full-time missionary service, but as someone once told me, "If it isn't heaven, it's a mission field," so wherever we are and whoever we are, the light of Christ can shine through us and our evangelistic heart!

[2] Cornelia Wieck's missionary biography can be found online at: http://new.gbgm-umc.org/work/missionaries/biographies/index.cfm?action=results&key=2&criteria=Wieck&Submit=Go. To read more of Wieck's missionary experiences, visit her blog: www.chinawieck.spaces.live.com.

My Reflections

Have you ever seen the presence of God shining through someone else as he or she went about doing a job, performing some task, or doing something that really wasn't "religious work" but nevertheless revealed the light of God in his or her life?

Have you ever had an experience when someone asked you why you cared or why you do what you do in such a caring way? How did you respond?

Day

3

Staying in the Neighborhood

*Jesus sent his twelve harvest hands out with this charge:
"Don't begin by traveling to some far-off place to convert unbelievers. And don't try to be dramatic by tack-
ling some public enemy. Go to the lost, confused people
right here in the neighborhood. Tell them that the kingdom is here." (Matthew 10:5-7,* The Message)

In a remote part of Minnesota, a church was struggling
to keep its doors open. (Imagine the movie *Fargo*, and
you have a pretty good idea what the characters in the
church were like—matter-of-fact, understated, and salt-of-
the-earth.) A pastor was sent to love and care for them and
also to help them discover their evangelistic hearts so that
they might reach out a little more.

They were somewhat skeptical even though they are loving
people. The pastor was pushing them a little to think of
reaching out verbally to share their faith. But they dutifully
listened and pondered it all in their hearts and minds.

One sunny afternoon, a regular life-long member of the church named Shirley was putting her groceries in the trunk of her car when she saw a young woman named Tiffany drive up next to her. As Tiffany got out of her car, Shirley greeted her and they began to talk. Shirley knew Tiffany's mother pretty well, but she didn't personally know Tiffany . . . other than what she had heard, which was what everyone else in the small town knew about Tiffany, too.

Shirley said to Tiffany, "I haven't seen you around in a while." Tiffany explained that her son, Jeremy, had been sick and with work and all, she hadn't gotten out much. Shirley imagined that it was hard for Tiffany being a single parent and working with a sick child. Suddenly Shirley remembered some things that she had been learning at church about inviting people in a gentle way to come to church.

Shirley asked Tiffany, "Do you have a church?" Tiffany looked at the ground and said, "I haven't gone to church much, since Jeremy was born." Neither one of them needed to say out loud what that meant—Tiffany didn't go to church because she wasn't married to Jeremy's father, and she was afraid how she would be treated. Or worse, how Jeremy would be treated.

Just about that time another young woman, Denise, who had recently been coming to Shirley's church drove up. Shirley hailed her over and introduced them. Denise and Tiffany had seen each other around but never met. Denise knew what everyone else in the town knew about Tiffany. They began to talk and discovered their children were about the same age.

After a while, Shirley asked Denise, "Denise, do you think Tiffany would like our church?" Shirley wasn't really asking Denise whether she thought Tiffany would like their type of music or the preacher or even the Sunday school program for her child; but all three of them knew that Shirley was asking Denise if Tiffany would be welcomed and accepted at their church even though everyone knew that Tiffany wasn't married to her son's father.

Denise enthusiastically said, "Oh, yes! Tiffany, you'd love coming to our church!" Denise continued to talk about the music, the preacher, and the Sunday school program, but in a way that made Tiffany know that this would be a safe place for her and her son to find support and encouragement in helping her face her issues in life.

Jesus' name was never used in the parking lot, but his love and grace were as present as the afternoon sun.

My Reflections

How were Shirley and Denise showing
the love and grace of Jesus to Tiffany?
Is that evangelism?

How do Shirley and Denise have evangelistic
hearts?

Day

4

Metaphors of Faith

Jesus told the crowds all these things in parables; without a parable he told them nothing. (Matthew 13:34)

I know an evangelism professor who emphasizes to his students that in order to share their faith they must find the right metaphor that connects with people. I've found this to be true, recognizing everyone has something in his or her life that can be used to explain the story of Jesus and his love.

One day a woman called me on the phone. I had officiated her mother's funeral a few months before. She wasn't a member of the church I was serving but had attended its preschool years before, so she turned to our church. This day she had a friend whose three-year-old child had died. Would I do the funeral for her? The family had no church connection at all.

Of course I would do the funeral. I met with the mother and she told me all about this wonderful little girl, Sunny, who

143

had died of cancer. Sunny had just returned from Disney World on a "Make a Wish" trip and was so excited to meet Buzz Lightyear there. Sunny, her mother told me, loved to go around saying, "To infinity and beyond!"

I smiled and nodded, but after they left, I went straight into the office of the children's minister of my church and asked, "Who is Buzz Lightyear?" He rolled his eyes and told me all about Buzz Lightyear, the hero of the children's movie *Toy Story*, which Sunny had watched over and over again in her short life.

If you, like me, don't have small children or grandchildren, you might not know that in the movie Buzz Lightyear is often frustrated because he is limited by being a plastic toy. However, even though he is limited by his physical powers, he brings peace and harmony, and his remarkable character reaches to "infinity and beyond."

No wonder Sunny was drawn to Buzz Lightyear. She knew she needed a savior, and he was as close to one as she had been given. She too was limited by her physical illness, but her character came through with love and joy.

I realized that I had one opportunity to convey the story of Jesus to Sunny's family and friends, most of who had no real knowledge of the love and grace of Jesus. With the help of my staff (who even supplied me with Buzz Lightyear action figures), I was able to tell the story of Jesus as our Savior who was limited by his humanity, suffered, and died for us so that we too can live "to infinity and beyond!"

My Reflections

What metaphor could you use to tell your own story of faith? How would you tell it to someone else?

Think about someone you'd like to share the love and grace of Jesus with in your life. What's their metaphor? How could you tell Jesus' story through that person's metaphor?

Day

5

Enlarge My Heart

Create in me a pure heart, O God,
and renew a steadfast spirit within me.
(Psalm 51:10, NIV)

When Mary sang out about the child who would be born into this world, she was rejoicing because people who were suffering—the least, lost, and left-out—would be the recipients of her good news. While her heart was magnifying the Lord and expanding with joy, it was also breaking for those who suffer because of physical, mental, spiritual, and even financial oppression.

Imagine someone or groups of people that need the love and grace of Jesus. Maybe you find it difficult to love them. Even if you don't, as you pray, let your soul be magnified—enlarged and stretched—with joy for who they are and what God can do in their lives through you.

How big is my heart?
Is it big enough to include another
Who is a child of God
But hard to love?

God, enlarge my heart
To love all your beloved children.
Especially enlarge my heart to love (name) _____.

How far can a heart be stretched?
Must my heart be stretched to love others
Who I don't like and find hard to love?
Why do you ask me to stretch my heart to love _____?

As my heart is grown and is stretched by your grace,
Help me to be more loving, more like Jesus,
Who must have had the biggest heart, stretched by the cross,
So that I can be near to the heart of God.
Thank you, O God! Amen.

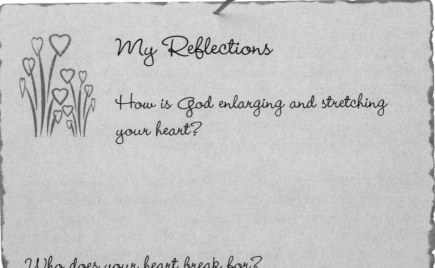

My Reflections

How is God enlarging and stretching your heart?

Who does your heart break for?

Day

6

Scattering Joy

"May the God of hope fill you with all joy and peace in believing, so that you may abound in hope by the power of the Holy Spirit." (Romans 15:13)

"Scatter joy," Ralph Waldo Emerson once said. An evangelistic heart scatters joy through word and deed.

When I was growing up, I had a cousin who was about fifteen years older than me. Her name was Leona, and she was a vacation Bible school teacher and camp leader when she was home for the summer. She would drive me and my other cousins to VBS or camp, which was over twenty miles from where we lived. Normally in our family this drive to church was one made in silence or minimal conversation; but with Leona, it was a joyful experience. She would lead us in singing or tell us funny stories, and we would laugh all the way to church. Laughing and singing were activities I associated with Leona and with her faith.

Leona became a missionary to the Hopi Indians and then later in Colombia, South America. For me she was an example of faith that stood in contrast to the way Christianity was often lived out in my early experiences. A "good" Christian was one who was somber and solemn. Leona's faith was marked by joy, laughter, and singing. She scattered joy everywhere she went; and as a young person, I wanted what she had!

An evangelistic heart is filled with joy that laughs and sings. A faith that "scatters joy" is the kind of faith that others are looking for in their lives because joy is contagious. I wanted the faith that brought joy to Leona's life.

My Reflections

How is God calling you to "scatter joy" today?

How have you experienced the contagious joy in another's faith?

Week

6

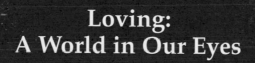

Loving:
A World in Our Eyes

Loving

Challenge for Week 6

On your own or as a group, find an
organization (local or international)
that needs your help. Ideas might be
to write letters of encouragement to
women who are in recovery from
domestic violence or drug abuse,
send care packages to children in
Third World countries, volunteer
locally, or contact your church for
additional ideas about organizations
they already support.

Week Six
Loving:
A World in Our Eyes

For God so loved the world . . . but do we? Jesus says that we're to be *in* the world but not *of* the world. Does that mean that we're not to love God's world?

Some sects such as the Amish have separated themselves from the world so the world doesn't corrupt them. Others, possibly including ourselves, may see the world as a strange and hostile place that eats away at our faith and way of life. Kathleen Norris describes how many rural communities and their peoples feel that the world brings change and conflict that destroys what they have known. They have

> a world view in which everything from the outside world is suspect, while everything local, especially that which derives from the immediate family, is good. These are families that have an exceptionally difficult time dealing with conflict and change. Change means failure; it is a contaminant brought in by outside elements.[1]

Our worlds constrict and expand according to our awareness and experience of the world. We know that our clothing and food come from all over the globe, and yet we don't feel very connected to those who make it or produce it. Our personal worlds constrict around us because increasingly, with the way our communities are constructed, we rarely see, much less know, our neighbors. And due to the "cyberworld" in which we live, we might know people better who live elsewhere in the country or even across the world. Now a world of people pops up on my Facebook page or in my inbox.

It used to be the standard question heard on a cell phone was, "Can you hear me now?" Now I find myself asking and being asked, "Where are you?" My family members joke and ask, "Where in the world is Aunt Sally?" So our world is both local and global, connected and disconnected in physical contact, fearful and unknown as well as intriguing and familiar.

Living within all of these worldviews, can it be that we can have jetlag of the soul as well as the body? Jetlag comes when we travel from one time zone to another so quickly that we don't have time to recover physically from the changes in sleeping and eating. Perhaps we have developed jetlag of the soul. We travel from one natural disaster in the world to another, causing us to be unable to muster the sympathy that the next one warrants.

Jesus loved the world enough to come and teach us how to live in it. Through our prayers and service we're called to love the world as intensely as Jesus loved it, willing to give and sacrifice so that people will know the love and grace of God, experience justice and peace, and have an environment that provides all the good things that God created.

[1] Kathleen Norris, *Dakota: A Spiritual Geography* (Houghton Mifflin, 1993); p. 84.

Day

1

Mary's Faithful Heart

Aware of the World's Needs

When [Jesus] came to Nazareth. . . . he stood up to read, and the scroll of the prophet Isaiah was given to him. He unrolled the scroll and found the place where it was written: "The Spirit of the Lord is upon me, because he has anointed me to bring good news to the poor. He has sent me to proclaim release to the captives and recovery of sight to the blind, to let the oppressed go free, to proclaim the year of the Lord's favor." (Luke 4:16-19)

*M*ary was aware of need in her life, community, and the world.

Though she would later become a refugee in Egypt (Matthew 2), before she was visited by the angel Gabriel, Mary had never ventured far from home. Still, when she received the news from Gabriel, she was deeply aware of people in need of One who would bring justice and mercy. When we read the words of her song, we read about a world that is in need of God's action:

And Mary said, ". . . Surely, from now on all generations will call me blessed; for the Mighty One has done great things for me, and holy is his name. His mercy is for those who fear him from generation to generation. He has shown strength with his arm; he has scattered the proud in the thoughts of their hearts. He has brought down the powerful from their thrones, and lifted up the lowly; he has filled the hungry with good things, and sent the rich away empty. He has helped his servant Israel, in remembrance of his mercy, according to the promise he made to our ancestors, to Abraham and to his descendants forever." (Luke 1:46-55)

The Sunday before Christmas one year, this passage from Luke was the selected Scripture for a church service. The pastor invited dialogue about the Scripture from those in attendance, and that particular morning, people had a lot of questions about Mary! One woman was visibly quite surprised to see such strong words coming out of "meek and mild" Mary. These were powerful words from an adolescent girl. But then, if you've ever had a conversation with a teenage girl, you might be convinced of their strong sense of justice and compassion for those in need, too. Mary sang of her son who would bring both mercy and justice, and therefore joy, to the world.

How aware of the world are we? In the words of Miriam Teichner, "God – let me be aware! / Stab my soul fiercely with others' pain."[2] Mary was aware of the world's needs, and she sang with the world on her heart.

[2] Miriam Teichner, "God – Let Me Be Aware!" in *Laughter, Silence, and Shouting: An Anthology of Women's Prayers*, compiled by Kathy Keay (Harper-Collins, 1994); p. 107.

My Reflections

When you were a teenager, what issues of justice were you passionate about?

If you know a teenager or have one in your family, what issues of justice are they passionate about?

Do you have a sense of justice toward a group of people, especially other than your own, that sparks passion in your soul? Why or why not?

Day

2

The World in Your Eye

*"For God so loved the world that he gave his only Son,
so that everyone who believes in him may not perish but
may have eternal life." (John 3:16)*

When Alice Walker, the author and poet, was a little girl, she was the apple of her father's eye. In fact, the whole family doted on her, and everyone remarked about how cute she was. She was outgoing and fun-loving.

This all changed one day when one of her brothers accidentally shot her in the eye with his BB gun. Afraid to tell their parents, treatment was delayed and then not adequately provided. Her eye developed a huge, ugly scar on it. She felt self-conscious and began to turn inward, and she started spending more time alone, writing stories and poems.

When she was older, a brother paid for eye surgery, but it left her with a small "bluish crater" where the scar tissue had been. While not perfect, it was an improvement, which gave her more self-confidence. She became more outgoing again.

Then when her daughter, Rebecca, was about three years old, while Alice was putting her down for a nap, her daughter's eyes locked onto her own. Alice cringed, waiting for whatever might be a child's honest reaction to her eye. Her daughter carefully studied her mother's eye, holding her mother's face in her hands. And then gently, with great interest, Rebecca asked, "Mommy, where did you *get* that world in your eye?"[3]

God so loved the world. Where did God get a world in God's own eye?

John Wesley said, "The world is my parish." Where did Wesley get a world in his eye?

The church is called to fulfill a global mission. Where did the church get a world in its eye?

[3] Alice Walker, *In Search of Our Mother's Gardens* (Harcourt, 1983); p. 370.

My Reflections

What about you? Do you have a world in your eye?

What part of the world grabs your heart as you see it groaning in pain and suffering?

How do you pray for the world?

Day

3

Praying With the World in Mind

"For if you love those who love you, what reward do you have? . . . And if you greet only your brothers and sisters, what more are you doing than others? Do not even the Gentiles do the same? Be perfect, therefore, as your heavenly Father is perfect." (Matthew 5:46-48)

The Talmud, an ancient rabbinic text, reads, "Never pray in a room without windows."

Never pray without the world in mind. Prayer is not intended to draw us away and out of the world, but draw us closer to it for the sake of God's own children. Some say that as Americans we can't bear that much reality and so we turn away. But I believe that our faith is what helps us to keep the world in our eye as we pray and serve.

Theologian Karl Barth is said to have instructed Christians during wartime to read with the Bible in one hand and the newspaper in the other.

Do you know what your church is doing for people in other parts of the world? I am able to see how The United

Methodist Church is at work throughout the world by visiting the websites of mission agencies like The United Methodist Committee on Relief[4] or The General Board of Global Ministries.[5] You might want to check to see how your church, denomination, or community is at work in the world.

Another way to pray for the world is to follow a prayer cycle, such as the one used by the World Council of Churches (WCC), which takes you on an annual around-the-world in prayer.[6] The WCC's prayer cycle, for example, provides a few countries to pray for each week and shares some concerns for those parts of the world. Through the indigenous prayers of the people who are Christian in those lands, you can pray your way around the world throughout the year.

Jesus calls us to pray even for people we don't know who live in places we're not familiar with and maybe couldn't even find on a world map! I grow discouraged when I attend churches that never mention the suffering of people that have been raised to our attention during the week in world news. The same people sitting in the pews of our churches may even talk about these events—natural disasters or human-created suffering, such as shootings, terrorism, etc.— at their places of work or even around the family dinner table, but they don't get mentioned in our corporate worship or in our personal prayers. Jesus expects that we will raise concerns for those we love, but what makes us any different from anyone else if we don't also pray for others in need?

---

[4] The United Methodist Committee on Relief: http://new.gbgm-umc.org/umcor/.
[5] The General Board of Global Ministries: http://new.gbgm-umc.org/.
[6] The World Council of Churches, weekly prayer cycle: http://www.oikoumene.org/en/resources/prayer-cycle.html.

My Reflections

Look at today's news, online or in print, and find an article about people in another part of the world who are suffering. Write a prayer for that part of the world that is in God's eye.

What does it feel like to pray for people you don't know?

What does it feel like to pray for people in extreme adversity when there might not be a lot you can do about it?

Day

4

Entering God's World

"This is the kind of fast day I'm after: to break the chains of injustice, get rid of exploitation in the workplace, free the oppressed, cancel debts. What I'm interested in seeing you do is: sharing your food with the hungry, inviting the homeless poor into your homes, putting clothes on the shivering ill-clad, being available to your own families. Do this and the lights will turn on, and your lives will turn around at once. Your righteousness will pave your way." (Isaiah 58:6-8, The Message)

We know the world, as God knows the world, only by entering it. Photos in *Newsweek* or *National Geographic* won't do. Editorials in *The Nation* or *The New Republic* won't do. Sixty-second clips on the nightly news about unemployment, homelessness, substance abuse, mental illness, and serial murderers won't do. You gotta *be* there.[7]

How can we *be* in the world? How can we enter the world the way God does?

Participating in mission is a way to enter God's world. Not everyone has the opportunity to travel to another place in the U.S. or world due to financial or life situations; but when we can, it can change our lives. When we enter God's world through mission, our world is never the same again and our horizons are forever widened.

I went on my first mission trip when I was fourteen. The church that I grew up in started a youth volunteer service, and I knew instantly that I wanted to go. I don't remember how I got the money to go, but I was always working and saving from the time I was very young, so I may have earned the money myself. The journey involved flying from Spokane, Washington, through O'Hare airport in Chicago. I had never been on a commercial flight before, much less alone in one of the busiest airports!

While on the mission trip, we worked in a hospital, caring for people much like one does in a Candy Striper program. At the time, I was thinking about becoming a nurse, so it was a helpful experience for me. We were trained to do a few practical things. But more importantly, I met people on this trip whose ideas about the world were different from mine. Or perhaps it would be better to say they had ideas and opinions about things that, until then, I hadn't spent much time thinking about. And after that experience, I spent a lot of time thinking about the war in Vietnam, poverty, and how people lived differently than I did.

I am sure that no one remembers our work on that mission trip. But as is usually the case on a mission trip, entering God's world left a huge imprint on *my* life. It's the way I got the world in my eye.

[7] Nancy Maris, "From My House to Mary's House," in *Storming Heaven's Gate: An Anthology of Spiritual Writings by Women*, edited by Amber Coverdale Sumrall and Patrice Vecchione (Plume, 1997); p. 156.

My Reflections

Have you ever been on a mission trip?
What was it like?

How do you feel about that part of the world as a result of going there and being with people through mission?

Day

5

Taking a Step Further

Learn to do right!
Seek justice,
*   encourage the oppressed.*
Defend the cause of the fatherless,
*   plead the case of the widow.*
*   (Isaiah 1:17, NIV)*

Genie Bank was the president of The United Methodist Women's Division from 2000–2004. On September 11, 2001, she and I were at a meeting just outside of New York City, and we spent the next two days—which seemed like a year—watching the news and wondering how we were going to get home. We finally got a car on the thirteenth and drove to Cleveland where she dropped me off, and then she headed on home to Michigan. We're forever bonded through that experience, as you can well imagine!

Genie is a beautiful, intelligent, and compassionate woman, who any of us would want to emulate. She is someone who "scatters joy" wherever she is and no matter what's going on in her life. I have great respect and admiration for Genie and her strong sense of love and mercy for those in need. She has lived out her calling in many ways because she has such an evangelistic heart. But she also has a world in her eye. Genie spoke to some women, affirming their acts of mercy (charity), but encouraging them to work for justice because she believes that,

> We need to see the difference between charity and justice. . . . I would suspect that . . . [you do] a bang-up job in the area of charity. Health kits and sewing kits and school kits and layettes are assembled and gathered for distribution to various places. Cans of food are collected for the food shelf in the community. You may go down to the soup kitchen to prepare and serve meals. Maybe you volunteer at your local school. And when the plate is passed, you manage to put in yet another dollar. [8]

See what I mean? She has an evangelistic heart and a world in her eye. But she challenges us to take it a step further and to step out of our comfort zone. While she says that such acts of charity are vital to being Christian, Genie says seeking justice is vital to being Christian, too.

> Christ was a justice seeker. . . . Even though people are fed and goods are distributed, nothing really changes. People remain hungry and homeless. Violence continues. There is still racism in our society. Children are without health care. Education remains under-funded. Air and water remain polluted. And the world knows no peace. . . . As Christians, ... we need to be advocates to change systems—systems that keep the poor poor, systems that

spend billions for the military and a fraction of that on health care and education.[9]

Genie challenges us to have a world in our eye that includes both acts of mercy—feeding the hungry, providing for children around the world, giving in all the ways that we do—and acts of justice—advocating for changes in our economic, political, and financial systems that keep people from being able to provide for themselves and their families.

Mercy and justice. Maybe it's like having a world in *each* eye! A world in one eye that looks to help those in need now, today—have mercy! And a world in the other eye that looks for solutions and systemic changes that keep people from being in need now, today—do justice!

[8] Genie Bank quoted in "From Charity to Justice" by Dana E. Jones, in *Response*, January-February 2004; p. 14.
[9] *Response*; p. 14.

My Reflections

Do you have a world in your eye?
In both eyes?

Which eye—mercy or justice—are you most inclined
to look through at your neighbor?

How could you "correct your vision" in the other eye?

Day

6

Care for Creation

God saw everything that he had made, and indeed, it was very good. (Genesis 1:31)

Part of God's world is creation itself. God created the heavens and the earth and all that is within them. God stated that creation was good, and for many of us it's in nature that we experience a closeness with God as well as a sense of God's mystery and wonder. Care for creation is part of our responsibility as people who call Earth our home. How do we treat our home?

A woman mystic of the eleventh century wrote these words:

> When I open my eyes,
> my God, on all that you have created
> I have heaven already in my hands.[10]

As we hold God's creation like "heaven in our hands," can we bear to pollute, waste, or destroy any part of it? I've had conversations about the environment with non-Christians. I've asked them, "What would Jesus do in terms of caring for creation?" Without a moment's hesitation, all of them instinctively believe that Jesus would recycle, care about creation, curtail consumption that tax the Earth's resources, and otherwise do whatever needs to be done to be good stewards of creation. Yet many Christians don't see any connection between caring for creation and living a Christian life. For many young people, they are disappointed, even disgusted, that the church doesn't lead the way in caring for creation.

Yet some believe that as Christians we need to make "ecology part of theology." The Council of Bishops of The United Methodist Church released a pastoral letter in December 2009. It begins with these words:

> God's creation is in crisis. We, the Bishops of The United Methodist Church, cannot remain silent while God's people and God's planet suffer. This beautiful natural world is a loving gift from God, the Creator of all things seen and unseen. God has entrusted its care to all of us, but we have turned our backs on God and on our responsibilities. Our neglect, selfishness, and pride have fostered:
>
> - pandemic poverty and disease,
> - environmental degradation, and
> - the proliferation of weapons and violence.
>
> Despite these interconnected threats to life and hope, God's creative work continues. Despite the ways we all contribute to these problems, God still invites each one of us to participate in the work of renewal. We must begin the work of renewing creation by being renewed in our

own hearts and minds. *We cannot help the world until we change our way of being in it.*[11]

God's creation is entrusted to us, just as our bodies are also entrusted to us. Having the "world in our eye" not only includes caring for those who live on the Earth, but also caring for the gift which God has given to us, the gift of Earth.

[10] Hildegard of Bingen, "Another Voice," in *Earth Gospel: A Guide to Prayer for God's Creation* by Sam Hamilton-Poore (Upper Room Books, 2008); p. 80. Permission to reprint granted by Liturgical Press, copyright © 1997.

[11] *God's Renewed Creation: Call to Hope and Action*, composed by the Council of Bishops of The United Methodist Church (Cokesbury, 2009, 2010); p. 5.

My Reflections

Open your eyes and look out upon nature. What do you see? Write down every living thing you can see and write a prayer of praise and thanksgiving for all the goodness of creation that you can see.

Do you think "ecology is part of theology"?

Do you see caring for creation as part of your
Christian discipleship? Why or why not?

What practices might you add to your life to care
for God's creation?

Week

7

Learning:
Discipleship as a
Lifelong Adventure

Learning

Challenge for Week 7

This week, go on an inward adventure following Jesus. Examine your own faith more deeply through spiritual practices such as prayer, Bible study, and small-group discussion. While on "adventure," make note of what demands courage, what challenges you, what gives you joy.

Week Seven
Learning: Discipleship as a Lifelong Adventure

I wish that throughout more of my life, especially as a young person, following Jesus had been presented as an adventure that you sign on for with full knowledge that you have no idea where this whole thing is going to lead you. Because that's exactly what happens when we follow Jesus, wherever and however he calls us!

Instead, following Jesus is presented, or at least was to me, as something that is going to keep you safe from all wrong and suffering and help you be a nice person. That's what you got—in addition to eternal life, of course—was being a nice person! Nice people didn't make waves or get into trouble. Nice people didn't really ever do anything bad, so what was there to confess and therefore be humble about? And once you know the story of Jesus—or even the gist of the whole Bible—who needed to make it part of one's daily life?

In fact, sometimes I wonder if author J.R.R. Tolkien wrote *The Hobbit* with Christians in mind. His description of hobbits sounds much like a Christianity that has been tamed by promising safety and values being nice.

The main hobbit, Bilbo Baggins, comes from a family of Bagginses that never had adventures and never did anything that was unexpected or surprising—hobbits who prided themselves in having orderly, quiet, unobtrusive, and predictable lives. After all, adventures disturb things, like your normal routines, and they make you do things that you wouldn't ever dream of doing which can be risky. Bilbo, like most hobbits, wanted to make sure he knew all the risks first: how much an adventure would cost and what the end outcome would be. But that's not really an adventure, is it?

But following Jesus *is* an adventure. An adventure is an exciting and sometimes dangerous undertaking. That said, if following Jesus had been presented to me as an adventure when I was young, I might have thought about making sure I was properly equipped with a prayer life that gave me courage and an understanding that being a follower might get me in trouble, the *right* kind of trouble—trouble like my baptismal vows suggested: resisting evil and injustice, loving my neighbor and my enemies, and picking up the cross and doing the hard things like speaking truth in love and all that. Following Jesus can be an adventure that requires everything from us, even our very lives.

Who'd sign up for something like that? Well, since risk is the world we live in, the biggest risk is *not* to sign up for the adventure in following Jesus where we experience God's love and grace along the way. Following Jesus is a lifelong adventure of learning what it means to be his disciple.

Day

1

Mary's Faithful Heart

Saying <u>Yes</u> to God

"No one lights a lamp, then hides it in a drawer. It's put on a lamp stand so those entering the room have light to see where they're going. Your eye is a lamp, lighting up your whole body. If you live wide-eyed in wonder and belief, your body fills up with light. If you live squinty-eyed in greed and distrust, your body is a dank cellar. Keep your eyes open, your lamp burning, so you don't get musty and murky. Keep your life as well-lighted as your best-lighted room." (Luke 11:33-36, The Message)

When the angel Gabriel came to Mary, the angel began by saying, "Do not be afraid!" The angel was telling Mary to "take heart," or have courage. The angel recognized that Mary would need courage just to talk to an angel, much less to do what God was calling her to do. She would need courage to say *Yes* to God and to live the rest of her life on the adventure of following her son, Jesus.

When Mary said *Yes* to the angel Gabriel, she was signing on for the journey of following Jesus, an adventure that would take her from the greatest joys to the deepest sorrows that humanity can experience. While she rejoiced in the Temple when she and Joseph presented Jesus to Simeon, he told her that her soul would be pierced by a sword, too (Luke 2:35). She didn't get to agree to the terms of being Jesus' mother; it was part of the adventure, as motherhood is. Did Mary have any idea that her son would grow up to heal the sick; raise the dead; teach the multitudes; or suffer, die, and be raised from the dead himself?

Evidence from Scripture suggests that Mary didn't know or fully understand the adventure that either she or her son was on. When Jesus as a child remained in Jerusalem to learn from the great teachers there, she was confused and pondered what it meant that he would be found there (Luke 2:41-51). What kind of son would he be? A great rabbi?

Yet it was Mary who pushed Jesus into his public ministry at the wedding feast in Cana (John 2:1-11). Jesus responded to his mother's request and the first miracle occurred! When Jesus began his public ministry, his family went out to hear him with the intent to "restrain him" because some people were saying he was out of his mind (Mark 3:19b-21)! Later when Jesus was told that Mary and his brothers and sisters were waiting to see him, he asked, "Who are my mother and my brothers? . . . Whoever does the will of God is my brother and sister and mother" (Mark 3:31-35). How does a mother feel when her own son broadens her family in such a way?

Mary followed Jesus to Jerusalem and was there when he was crucified. When the shepherds came and the angels sang over her child, she could never have imagined the journey would take her to the agony of the cross or the joy of his resurrection and the assurance of her own heavenly resurrection.

Mary represents a model of discipleship and adventure for all Christians, but particularly for those of us who have been in the Christian family most of our lives. We might not have big dramatic conversion stories, but like Mary our lives are an ever-widening experience, journeying and sometimes detouring in our faith, and coming to places along the adventure that we would never have imagined for ourselves. Sometimes it's a journey of sorrowful tears and sometimes it's a journey of laughter and joy that we would never have known unless our family was broadened by the church.

Part of life's adventure is experiencing the suffering that comes from being human and loving others. Mary has become a source of comfort for women who suffer around the world, especially in countries where Catholicism is the dominant religion. Her suffering, or *pietà*, is symbolized by a picture or statue of her holding her dead son's body on her lap. For many that image is a way of describing the church holding the suffering of the world. One woman remarked,

> When my oldest son died, one of my few comforting insights during the disruption and long sorrow this event caused our whole family was that Mary, too, had been through such a tragedy. I no longer saw Pietàs, in which the mother holds the body of her son across her knees, as simply pious images; they became representations of a completely human woman who shared the pain of all mothers—all parents—who have lost their children.[1]

[1] Sally Cunneen, *In Search of Mary: The Woman and the Symbol* (Ballantine Books, 1996); p. 14.

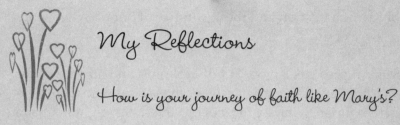

My Reflections

How is your journey of faith like Mary's?

How is it different?

Would you describe Mary's journey with Jesus to be an adventure?

Is your journey with Jesus an adventure?

Have you ever connected with Mary's suffering?

Day 2

Crossing Your "Atlantics"

For I am the LORD, your God,
who takes hold of your right hand
and says to you, Do not fear;
I will help you. (Isaiah 41:13, NIV)

Amelia Earhart was a woman of adventure. She demonstrated great courage in the early days of flying, breaking many stereotypes and barriers for women. She once said, "The love of flying is the love of beauty. It was more beautiful up there than anything I had known."[2] An adventure involves both beauty and courage. In following Jesus, we encounter the beauty of God's goodness and grace in our lives, but we also face experiences that require courage.

Earhart waxed philosophic and helped us to see that while she flew planes, we all have our own "Atlantics" to cross:

My particular inner desire to fly the Atlantic alone was nothing new with me. I had flown Atlantics before. Everyone has [her] own Atlantics to fly. Whatever you want very much to do, against the opposition of tradition, neighborhood opinion, and so-called "common sense"—that is an Atlantic. . . . I flew the Atlantic because I wanted to. . . . To want in one's heart to do a thing, for its own sake; to enjoy doing it; to concentrate all one's energies upon it—that is not only the surest guarantee of success. It is also being true to oneself.[3]

[2] Virginia Morell, "Amelia Earhart," in *National Geographic*, January 1998; p. 135.
[3] *National Geographic*; p. 130.

My Reflections

What's your "Atlantic" in life?

How has your faith adventure helped you see both the beauty of humanity and the world by following Jesus as well as find the courage to face it?

Day

3

Following Jesus

As [Jesus] walked by the Sea of Galilee, he saw two brothers, Simon, who is called Peter, and Andrew his brother. . . . And he said to them, "Follow me."
(Matthew 4:18-19)

Dorothy, my father's cousin, is now in her nineties. She was my Sunday school teacher many times over, from the time I was born until I was a youth. She was always the one who could be counted on to bring food to a funeral or feed the multitudes when there was a big church dinner. She must have rolled miles of bandages to send to cancer patients in those days. She was the one who made quilts to give to the poor or sell to raise money for mission work. Her list of service spans her ninety years and is far more detailed than I could ever remember.

But when she was eighty-four she wanted to go on an adventure that she had never had the opportunity to take. She had sent countless members of her family and church on mission trips over the years, including me when I was fourteen, but she had never really gone on a mission trip herself!

There was always something that was too big of an obstacle, such as family concerns or health. But following Hurricane Katrina, she said her time was running out to do something and she wanted to go on a mission, to have an adventure of helping others.

Still she was a little uncertain and wavering, but her daughter bought the plane ticket as quickly as she could, knowing her mother wouldn't back out if money had been spent. Dorothy's grandson decided to go, too, and that gave her a sense of comfort. Dorothy prayed for good health for the trip and that she "wouldn't be a burden to anyone."

Dorothy went. She didn't swing hammers or repair roofs, but she did what she is known for in several states: she cooked. In the kitchen where the mission teams stayed, Dorothy cooked breakfast, packed lunches, and prepared evening meals. While she was at it, she even cleaned up the kitchen so that those who ran the place said that it was cleaner than they'd ever seen it!

Dorothy also talked to everyone, making them feel welcome, whether they were on the mission team or having work done on their homes after Katrina. She was thrilled with her adventure in following Jesus. Her life was made richer as a result of her experience. She came to appreciate how hard it must be to lose everything—your home, possessions, clothes, keepsakes, everything. And she is all the more grateful not only for what she has but also for the opportunity for such an adventure in following Jesus.

My Reflections

What have you always wanted to do in following Jesus?

What keeps you from doing it?

What would it take to be on that adventure with Jesus that helps you see the beauty, but also requires the courage of faith?

Day

4

Exploring Your Faith—
Have You Begun?

*"Surely I am with you always, to the very end
of the age." (Matthew 28:20, NIV)*

Adventures occur when we do things, such as go on mission trips, but there are also adventures of the mind and spirit. In one of the churches I served there was, and continues to be, a weekly Bible study for elderly women. Every week, they study the Scriptures and examine their lives through the passage. They've read book after book of the Bible over the years, many of them over and over again.

One particular day after the Bible study, I went into the kitchenette to check on something for their lunch afterward and found one of the women there, who was eighty years old at the time, and she was crying. When I asked why she was crying, she told me that she had never really understood the Scriptures before and it felt like her faith had been unexamined all those years. "How do you begin when you're eighty?" she asked. Though my words didn't sound like much comfort in the moment, I said, "At least you've begun." She began the adventure when she became aware of the beauty and courage needed to get on board.

Earlier in this study, I told of three women of different faiths. When the three women—a Muslim, a Christian, and a Jew—came together to write a book, they discovered that they not only learned about each other's faiths, but about their own as well. Each found her faith to be deepened by the experience. Their "faith club" was an adventure of the mind and spirit. As Suzanne Oliver, the Christian in the triad, says,

> It was through my own discussions with a Muslim and a Jew that I was beginning to understand my Christian soul in a way I never had before. In talking with two people of other faiths, everything I believed had been called into question. Every assumption was up for examination and debate. I never would have plumbed my faith to the extent I had if I had not been in this conversation. . . . I had begun to understand what was vital in my own [faith].[4]

Exploring her faith raised more questions than gave answers. It was unsettling, even disturbing, at times to think about what it means to be a Christian and to be in relationship with people who weren't of her faith. Yet it was the most enriching experience of her life.

Following Jesus isn't for the faint-hearted, is it? Yet following Jesus is an adventure that pushes us deeper toward God within us and stretches us outwardly toward our neighbors.

[4] *The Faith Club*; p. 217.

My Reflections

Have you ever gone on an inward adventure following Jesus, being pushed to examine your faith more deeply through prayer, Bible study, small-group discussion, or exploration of others' beliefs?

What was it like? What took courage?

How was your life disturbed?

What gave you joy?

Day

5

A Daring Adventure

[The Master] said, "That's what I mean: Risk your life and get more than you ever dreamed of. Play it safe and end up holding the bag." (Luke 19:26, The Message)

*C*onsider a woman whose life was an adventure without sight or sound, but who transformed the lives of others forever.

Security is mostly a superstition. It does not exist in nature, nor do the children of [humanity] as a whole experience it. Avoiding danger is no safer in the long run than outright exposure. Life is a daring adventure or nothing at all.

—Helen Keller

If life is a daring adventure, then it takes courage to live a life of faith. The word *courage* comes from the same French word that means "heart." Just as one's heart pumps blood into one's arms, legs, and brain so that one can function, so courage makes possible all the other Christian virtues of faith, hope, and love. Courage is the blood supply of faith. We don't talk about courage much in our culture. I can't remember anyone telling me when I was growing up that I would need courage or to "have courage." But I soon learned that it takes courage in life and faith to be faithful to God's calling.

It took courage for me as an adolescent to go on my first mission trip. Courage was necessary to be the first one in my family to attend college. More courage was necessary when I chose to go to college all the way across the country. More and more courage was required to answer a call to ministry in the 1970's when women in ministry were still pretty rare. Courage was essential to face the day to day demands of an urban church in the midst of gang violence, prostitution, and pornography theaters. Courage is needed whenever clergy move from one church to another (and courage is even needed to receive a new pastor). Everyday courage must pump life into my faith and hope as I seek to bring leadership in the midst of the many challenges to the church today.

Likewise it takes courage not to despair at the many threats to our national security, our environment, and our economy. Where do we find the courage to even wake up in the morning?

Again, *courage* finds its roots in the French word for *heart*. It takes courage to live faithfully instead of securely; there are no guarantees in life and in the midst of the uncertainties that life brings, courage keeps us focused on our faith in God.

Discipleship is not for the faint-hearted, either. When everything in our culture is changing, following Jesus requires that we not have a spirit of timidity (2 Timothy 1:7) but one of courage to challenge injustice, to love the unlovely, to live with hope.

With changes in our churches and fewer people turning to the church, we must have courage to take risks and experiment with new ways of reaching people with the gospel. There are no certainties that our investments in time and money will pan out, but with courage we take risks and sometimes we find that they are fruitful—and as a result people take their own leaps of faith into a life in Christ and a faith community.

A life of discipleship is a daring adventure—one that is lived fully and freely in the assurance of our hope in Christ Jesus.

My Reflections

How is a marriage a daring adventure?

How is being single a daring adventure?

How is raising a child a daring adventure?

How do these "common" but daring relationships teach us the beauty and draw from us the courage to live our lives as an adventure with each other and Jesus?

Day

6

Where Will the Way Lead?

"Trust in the LORD with all your heart,
and do not rely on your own insight."
(Proverbs 3:5)

Following Jesus is a lifetime adventure. It requires risk and experimentation. Courage is necessary to increase our faith, hope, and love along the journey. We don't know what life will bring to us—surprises that both overwhelm us with joy and sorrow.

So how do we know the way? A long time ago I heard a story that I've contemplated many times in my life when I didn't know where the path I was on would lead. The story goes as I remember it like this: One night a father decided that his daughter was old enough to go to the barn and feed the horses on her own. But she was afraid.

So the father took his daughter out to the front porch of the house and lit a lantern, held it up, and asked her how far she could see by the lantern's light. She said that she could see halfway down the path to the barn. "Good!" her father responded. "Now carry this lantern halfway down the path." The young girl did as she was told and when she reached her destination, her father called out to her, "Now how far can you see by the lantern's light?" His daughter responded that she could see all the way to the gate. "Great!" her father responded. "Now walk to the gate."

Once again the girl did as she was told and when she reached the gate, her father asked, "Now how far can you see?" She responded that she could see the barn. "Wonderful!" replied her father. "Now walk to the barn and open the door."

The girl did just as her father told her and finally she shouted back that she was at the barn and could see the horses. "Excellent!" her father called. "Now feed the horses." And he stepped back into the house.

God is like the father who gives us light for now and for the next step. God's light doesn't illuminate the whole journey, just one step at a time. The girl trusted her father to get her safely to the barn; and we, too, must trust God to get us safely to the next destination, decision, turning point, opportunity, or experience along our path.

My Reflections

When you are uncertain of the path ahead,
how do you trust to take the next steps?

Write a prayer confessing your uncertainty of where the way will lead. Be honest about where you feel doubt and where you feel hope along the journey.

Week

8

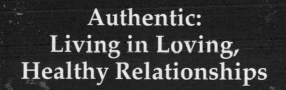

Authentic:
Living in Loving,
Healthy Relationships

Authentic

Challenge for Week 8

This week, practice forgiveness. Think of a hurt you are holding onto, and imagine you are looking at the person(s) who hurt you through "forgiveness glasses"—with new eyes. Write your own prayer for the person(s) who wronged you.

Week Eight
Authentic: Living in Loving, Healthy Relationships

My big, audacious dream and hope for faith communities is that they teach us how to have healthy relationships. In community we can be "re-parented." My home church was a place where other adults—usually relatives and friends of my parents—would teach me, mentor me, and help me imagine other ways of being and experiencing faith than what two parents can provide. It takes a church to raise a person who has experienced healthy relationships.

In community we learn to forgive others and to love our enemies. Forgiveness and loving our enemies don't usually happen when we are left to our own natural instincts. How do we observe people living and loving together through the bumps in the road in such a way that we understand the benefit and are taught how to do it? It takes a church to raise us to have healthy relationships!

In community we learn to love our neighbors—those near and far. Through community we are invited, encouraged, pushed, and pulled to find ways of seeing God in the faces of those who we serve and come to know as our brothers and sisters in Christ. Like families, we don't get to pick and choose our brothers and sisters in Christ!

While families can teach us many things about loving, healthy relationships, it is through community that we learn to engage in loving, healthy relationships with a variety of people throughout the dynamic experiences of life.

Complicated Relationships

"Make this your common practice: Confess your sins to each other and pray for each other so that you can live together whole and healed." (James 5:16, The Message)

Mary had some complicated relationships. She was betrothed to Joseph, who, when he found out she was pregnant, planned to quietly divorce her. That was a kind solution, as opposed to publicly stoning her, which was his jilted right. I wonder if, when Jesus encountered the woman caught in adultery (John 8:1-11), he might have thought how that could have been his mother had God not intervened? Somehow Mary navigated an historical phenomenon in her relationship with Joseph.

Mary's relationship with Jesus was also complicated. As we read earlier, Mary both encouraged Jesus in his public ministry as in the story of the miracle at Cana (John 2:1-11) and seemed at times to think, like other members of the family, that he was out of his mind (Mark 3:21). Like any mother, she both supported and wondered about her child.

Mary's relationships became more complicated when Jesus "gave her away" to the disciple John (John 19:26-27). Some traditions hold that after Jesus' crucifixion and resurrection, she went with John to Ephesus where she lived out the rest of her life. If this is true, then cut off from family members back home in Nazareth or from friends she knew with Jesus in Jerusalem, she would have started a new life. Jesus' question, "Who is my mother, and who are my brothers?" (Matthew 12:48), may have come home to rest as a blessed assurance in her heart as she realized that without a broadened understanding of family through Jesus, she would have been left all alone. She was in a community of faith.

My Reflections

What are the complicated relationships in your life?

How do they match the complications that Mary had in her relationships?

What could you learn from Mary?

What have you learned from your faith community in terms of healthy relationships?

Day

2

The Radical Role of Forgiveness

"Be kind to one another, tenderhearted, forgiving one another, as God in Christ has forgiven you."
(Ephesians 4:32)

Whether it's toward our best friend, spouse, fellow church member, a stranger who hurts us, or even God, forgiveness is probably one of the most difficult tasks in relationships. Jesus taught about forgiveness, giving his life to assure us that we are forgiven so that we will forgive others. His teaching is clear and yet we resist the power of forgiveness in our lives and faith.

Recently, I heard on the radio about a documentary entitled *The Power of Forgiveness* by Martin Doblmeier (also a book by Kenneth Briggs, based on the film). It explores the radical and central role of forgiveness in our Christian faith and raises some concepts that may come as a surprise to us when we don't expect forgiveness to be taught in our churches or made central in our faith.

You may recall that in 2006 there was a shooting of children at an Amish school in Pennsylvania. Almost immediately following the shootings, the Amish gave a public statement of forgiveness. Doblmeier's documentary reveals that the extension of forgiveness wasn't made by the immediate family members of the children who were killed but rather by the Amish community—forgiveness wasn't an individual act but a *communal* act of reconciliation. The community is stronger than the individual for the Amish. In the Amish community, it is the *expectation* that the community will come to the place of forgiveness as individuals move toward that end on their own path and timetable.

The Amish have the advantage of living in a community that teaches forgiveness, generation to generation, so that individuals aren't left wondering what to do with all the pain.

My Reflections

When someone hurts you, do you expect that you will get to a place of forgiveness toward that person?

With or without that person's help? With or without the help of a community of faith?

What's the hardest thing you've ever had to forgive? Where did you get the strength to do it?

What if we were a people known to be a community of forgiveness and reconciliation?

Day

3

Wearing Forgiveness Glasses

*"Welcome with open arms fellow believers who don't see
things the way you do. And don't jump all over them
every time they do or say something you don't agree
with—even when it seems that they are strong on opinions but weak in the faith department. Remember, they
have their own history to deal with. Treat them gently. . . .
So where does that leave you when you criticize a
brother? And where does that leave you when you con-
descend to a sister? I'd say it leaves you looking pretty
silly—or worse. Eventually, we're all going to end up
kneeling side by side in the place of judgment, facing
God. Your critical and condescending ways aren't going
to improve your position there one bit."*
(Romans 14:1, 10-11, The Message)

$\mathcal{F}$orgiveness comes because we have been taught to forgive. Sometimes the teaching hasn't been helpful because it insists that we get to the place of forgiveness way
before we're ready. That shoves the pain down deeper with
nothing to tap its oozing resentment. Like a festering sore, it
becomes infected within our spirits.

Being taught to forgive means that we have the opportunity to *see* how people forgive those who have hurt them. We see forgiveness occur in our families, hopefully around minor situations as we grow up, so that we can apply the process of forgiveness to bigger things. We watch people say they're sorry and learn when people mean it. We learn to say we're sorry and to know when we mean it. We experience the pain of forgiveness and the healing that comes because of it.

The Doblmeier documentary, *The Power of Forgiveness*, mentioned in the reading for Day 2 of this week, tells the story of a school system in Belfast, Northern Ireland, where they were teaching the practice of forgiveness in a culture that has been divided and fraught with inflicted pain on all sides.

First, the students are asked about a transgression in their lives, something that a brother or sister might have done to upset or hurt them. Then they give the students "forgiveness glasses"—neon-colored glasses—and tell them to "see" or imagine the person who hurt them with new eyes. The children put on the glasses as a symbol or demonstration of how one must look at the world differently and try to see others with new eyes.

As a result, they admit that their brother or sister hurt them but also acknowledge what a sibling does that is good, like being there for them when needed. Obviously, this lesson in forgiveness doesn't end all the deep hostility in Northern Ireland, but it begins to ask the question whether we can, in fact, see a situation differently and both expect and practice forgiveness.

Kenneth Briggs, the author of the book based on the documentary, was asked how this project on forgiveness has changed his life. He laughed and said, "It [has] just made my life more difficult. . . . I'm not allowed to avoid these things quite to the extent that I might once have been able to do."[1] Forgiveness didn't used to be on his radar screen; it wasn't a part of his faith commitment, but after working on this project and focusing on forgiveness, he saw that forgiveness is central to what it means to be a follower of Jesus.

A consequence of following Jesus is having the will to forgive others.

[1] Interviewed on Interfaith Voices, aired March 27, 2008; available: http://Interfaithradio.org/node/400.

My Reflections

How were you taught to forgive—or not to forgive?

What do you think a healthy apology is? When have you experienced one?

Have you seen forgiveness as a central part of your faith commitment? Why or why not?

Day

4

Help Us Accept Each Other

*"I'm telling you to love your enemies. Let them bring
out the best in you, not the worst. When someone gives
you a hard time, respond with the energies of prayer, for
then you are working out of your true selves, your God-
created selves. This is what God does. . . . If all you do is
love the lovable, do you expect a bonus? Anybody can do
that. If you simply say hello to those who greet you, do
you expect a medal? Any run-of-the-mill sinner does
that. In a word, what I'm saying is, Grow up. You're
kingdom subjects. Now live like it. Live out your God-
created identity. Live generously and graciously toward
others, the way God lives toward you."*
(Matthew 5:44-48, The Message)

Jesus taught that we are to be in right relationship with others. A right relationship is a relationship of love and forgiveness, even if the other person is our enemy. Jesus' commandments are to love God and our neighbor; we don't have one without the other. They are two sides of the same coin; and if you only have one side of a coin, you don't have a coin at all!

One of my favorite hymns is "Help Us Accept Each Other," which says,

> Teach us to care for people, for all, not just for some,
> To love them as we find them, or as they may become.[2]

These lines and the Scripture above speak of an inclusive love, one that welcomes all people, not just those we like or who are like us. What if we acted like the Scripture says, and let our enemies bring out the best in us, not the worst? We are to love and accept those with whom we are in relationship, only then are we acting as "our God-created selves."

Let us pray:

Lord, for today's encounters with all who are in need,
Help me to love others as who they might become
Instead of the one whose shortcomings are ever before me.
Give me new eyes for seeing _____ (fill in a name or group)
And new hands for holding onto the hope of true forgiveness and reconciliation.

I pray for others who are in conflict around me:
Renew them with your Spirit, Lord, free them, and make them one!
I pray for the world which is divided by all the differences that humanity can manifest.
Teach us to care for people, for all, not just for some;

Teach me to care for people I'll never meet
and who live on the other side of town or the world
But are in need of my love and help.
Broaden the human family with love and forgiveness,
Beginning with me.

In Jesus' name I pray, Amen.

[2] "Help Us Accept Each Other," words by Fred Kaan, in *The United Methodist Hymnal* (The United Methodist Publishing House, 1989); p. 560.

My Reflections

Find the hymn "Help Us Accept Each Other" in a hymnal or online, and read the lyrics.

What do you find comforting about these lyrics?

Which words or phrases do you find challenging, even uncomfortable?

What does this hymn say about a difficult relationship you are in right now?

What does this hymn say about a faith community that doesn't always live up to the one that Jesus envisioned for us?

Day

5

Paradoxical Commandments

"In everything do to others as you would have them do to you." (Matthew 7:12)

For years while the "Ask Ann Landers" advice column still ran, a poem entitled "Anyway" would appear periodically. Over the years, I clipped the poem out almost every time because the words always struck me as some of the best advice on how to live our lives.

My yellowed copies reveal that the author of the poem was always listed as "anonymous," but over time it was attributed to Mother Teresa, who evidently had a copy among her things when she died. But in September 1997, following Mother Teresa's death, a man by the name of Kent Keith was at his Rotary Club meeting. A fellow Rotarian commented on the passing of Mother Teresa and proceeded to read a poem she had written. As Kent Keith bowed his head, he heard the words he had written thirty years before. He went to a bookstore and found a book with the words credited to

Mother Teresa. There were his words, reformatted to look like a poem with no author listed; at the bottom it said, "From a sign on the wall of the children's home in Calcutta."[3]

Later, he told how he had written these words in 1968 when he was a sophomore at Harvard—words written to encourage high school students during the 1960's to keep working through the system to bring about change. He had seen students give up because they had high hopes and ideals but when they received negative feedback or suffered failure, they just quit, dropped out, and stopped trying. He calls these the "Paradoxical Commandments":

People are illogical, unreasonable, and self-centered.

LOVE THEM ANYWAY.

If you do good, people will accuse you of selfish ulterior motives.

DO GOOD ANYWAY.

If you are successful, you will win false friends and true enemies.

SUCCEED ANYWAY.

The good you do today will be forgotten tomorrow.

DO GOOD ANYWAY.

Honesty and frankness make you
vulnerable.

BE HONEST AND FRANK ANYWAY.

The biggest men and women
with the biggest ideas
can be shot down by the
smallest men and women
with the smallest minds.

THINK BIG ANYWAY.

People favor underdogs
but follow only top dogs.

FIGHT FOR A FEW UNDERDOGS ANYWAY.

What you spend years building
may be destroyed overnight.

BUILD ANYWAY.

People really need help
but may attack you if you do help them.

HELP PEOPLE ANYWAY.

Give the world the best you have
and you'll get kicked in the teeth.

*GIVE THE WORLD THE BEST YOU HAVE
ANYWAY.*

[3] Kent M. Keith, *Anyway: The Paradoxical Commandments: Finding Personal Meaning in a Crazy World* (G.P. Putnam's Sons, 2001).

My Reflections

Which one of these "paradoxical commandments" applies the most to you and your
relationships right now?

What does this "commandment" teach you about how
to live your life and faith?

Day

6

Three Simple Rules

*Jesus answered, "The first is, '. . . you shall love the Lord
your God with all your heart, and with all your soul,
and with all your mind, and with all your strength.' The
second is this, 'You shall love your neighbor as yourself.'
There is no other commandment greater than these."*
(Mark 12:29-31)

John Wesley provided three practical but admittedly difficult rules to help us sort through our own lives with a
discerning eye toward good and healthy relationships with
God and others.

Do no harm, do good, and stay in love with God.[4]

Avoiding harm can be as small (but as difficult) as holding our
tongue when a stranger walks into our church with tattoos
all over his or her body; or it might be putting into place a re-
cycling system at work, home, or church.

Doing good means we proactively and intentionally seek to
help, care, love, forgive, and do justice where the opportunity arises.

Staying in love with God is to fully love God by practicing spiritual disciplines that shape our hearts and minds to become more Christ-like so we can practice the first two rules of doing no harm and doing good toward others.

These three simple rules are interconnected and keep us moving toward God and others in a healthy way.

[4] Rueben P. Job, *Three Simple Rules: A Wesleyan Way of Living* (Abingdon Press, 2007).

My Reflections

At the end of each day, what if we reviewed our actions and attitudes with the three simple rules of Wesleyan living?

How do these three simple rules help us to have loving, healthy relationships?

How might I avoid doing harm, do good, and stay in love with God tomorrow?

Epilogue

As you read, journaled, pondered, and discussed *A Faithful Heart*, I hope that you have been able to see the great cloud of faithful hearts that surround you through the example of Mary, the other women described, and those in your daily life. Mostly, I hope that you have become more aware and strengthened in your confidence that you have a faithful heart that is:

> *Passionate*
> *Called*
> *Holy*
> *Equipped*
> *Joyful*
> *Loving*
> *Learning*
> *Authentic*

While some of the characteristics of a faithful heart may stand out more than others as you ponder your own life and observe the lives of others, remember that a faithful heart comes through practicing daily the "cardio exercises" that draw us closer to God and help us live a joyful life in Christ.

May God bless you and your faithful heart!

Sally Dyck

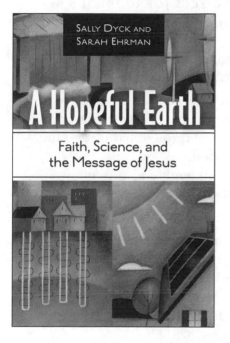